The Warrior's Agenda Combat Study Guide For Lead Warriors...

David M. Humphrey, Sr.

Copyright © 2005 by David M. Humphrey, Sr.

The Warrior's Agenda Combat Study Guide For Lead Warriors...
by David M. Humphrey, Sr

Printed in the United States of America

ISBN 1-59781-466-0

All rights reserved solely by the author. The author guarantees all contents are original and do not infringe upon the legal rights of any other person or work. No part of this book may be reproduced in any form without the permission of the author. The views expressed in this book are not necessarily those of the publisher.

Unless otherwise indicated, Bible quotations are taken from the King James Version. Copyright © 1991 by Dake Bible Sales.

www.xulonpress.com

The Warrior's Agenda Combat Study Guide:

Learning How To Be *Combat Effective*

In Spiritual Warfare...

God's Principles of Spiritual Self-Defense:

For Your Home, Your Family, Your Vision, Your Life and Your Ministry...

Part 1

Acknowledgements

To my Sons, Brian, Eric and David Jr., I love you much, you make me proud...

To My Wife, Velma, who's constant prayers, encouragement and support has been used by the Lord to help me complete each challenging project He's given me to do...

To (Gen.) Curry Blake: A Friend Who's More Than a Friend, A Mentor Who's More Than A Mentor, A Brother, A Leader, A True Man of God

To (Col.) Everrett Hall: Ho! My Friend! Thanks for the encouragement, the support and for being more than a Brother under fire. To a true **_Brother in Arms_** and the Best Partner in the World in **_Shadow Ops_**...

To Elya and Jerice Williams: I love you guys and thank you so much for your support during the hard years. Thanks Si-hing. Thank God for you and Everrett. Two Warriors who never believed in leaving a wounded soldier behind...

Dedication

To the brave men and women of our Armed Forces around the world. Especially, those who serve in our Special Forces, whose determination, dedication and self-sacrifice set a powerful and compassionate example for us all…

De Opresso Liber …

Table of Contents

Forward………………………………………1

Not A Clue…………………………………...2

Chapter 1- Like Spiritual Kung Fu………………..6

Chapter 2- Spiritual Boxing……………………..15

Chapter 3- Skill Builders…………………….…..26

Chapter 4- Only Forward-Never Back……………36

Chapter 5- The Warrior Mind Set…………………54

Forward

Welcome to the Warrior's Training School, otherwise known as The War College…

Welcome to Special Forces Training Camp number 4719. One of many that our Heavenly Father is raising up in these days to not just *teach* His people, but to *train them* in the art of Spiritual Warfare and the realities of Spiritual Combat.

God is tired of Satan running over His people. *He's* tired of it even if *we're* not. Psalm 105:14 & 15, Num. 23:8, 11,19,20,24-26, Num. 24:9.

Exodus 15:3 says that "The Lord is a Man of War", KJV. Another translation puts it this way:

"The Lord is a Warrior…"

Well, like the old saying goes, 'the apple don't fall far from the tree…' and 'like father, like son, (or daughter…')

Hmmm, well if that's true--and it is, then what does that make <u>you</u>?

You guessed it.
Welcome to Warrior Training 101…

Not a Clue…

Paul made a very profound statement in 2nd Corinth. 2:11.

"Lest Satan should get an advantage over us: for we are not ignorant of his devices."

Are *you*?

Too many believers in the Body of Christ *are* ignorant of Satan's devices. Why? Because too many in the Body don't *study* the only Book in the world that can *prevent* them from being ignorant of his devices…

The word for 'devices' in the Greek can also be translated "purposes".

We must not be ignorant of Satan's purposes, nor of the manner in which he endeavors to work against us. The Word teaches us *how* he strikes and some of the finer points of his devices. Sadly, the *majority* of the Body of Christ has been woefully ignorant and without a clue. And there are divorce courts, hospitals, graveyards, psychiatrist couches, and mental wards full of Christians, unfortunately, to prove it...

The following material will be concise, specific, dynamic, scriptural, and to the point.

This information and material will assist the mature Christian in becoming more combat effective in their individual warfare, and thus more effective as a *team*. You may have encountered a sticking point regarding an area of healing, finances, emotional challenges, believing for loved ones, etc. Though we vary as individuals the one common denominator is, sooner or later we find ourselves face to face and challenged in our lives and needing to confront one or more of these particular works of the enemy.

This course treats the Word of God as what it is—practical, powerful and life changing. What makes this course different is the fact that it approaches the conflict stage of your Christian life as what it is—***Warfare.*** If for one moment you forget the fact that this is a real **WAR** that we are engaged in, you will pay the price, or worse, those who depend upon you could.

This course will approach spiritual conflict therefore from a "*combat effective*" model. We will approach this warfare from both a **military model** and a **martial arts** model.

    A. The information you will learn is for your own spiritual self-defense.

    B. We will examine the military mode from a Special Forces point of view.

C. You will be trained and encouraged to actually 'apply' what you have learned. Not just sit on it.

Neither we nor anyone else can be your 'Holy Spirit'. The Lord has only One, and nobody can take His place, meaning this is a course where **you** will learn the **responsibility** of listening to the Holy Spirit for your***self***. **YOU** will have to spend time in personal prayer. **YOU** will have to spend time reading the Word of God. **YOU** will have to spend time studying the Word of God. And **YOU** will have to spend time meditating in the Word of God for yourself. We can, and will, show you effective ways of doing that, but you must remember, we are not Old Testament saints, but ***New Testament*** ones. We don't keep sending some one inside the tabernacle over and over again to keep getting our individual answers *for* us, and telling us every *little* thing we should do.

The Word teaches that we are each Kings and Priests before God now, (Rev.1:5&6, 5:10 KJV) and have the right and *responsibility* to daily seek God in prayer for ourselves, and He will hear us.

Thank God for our Pastors, but they will be among the first to tell you, that there comes a time that **you** have to study, pray, read, meditate and act on the Word of God for your*self.* That's what makes a *mature* Christian.

Now, let's get to work.

Let's begin with the Martial Arts Model Phase of our course...

Understanding the *Ways* of Your Enemy...

Satan attacks in 3 Ways (See Psalm 91:13)
1. **Like a Lion--An Aggressive Bold Attack**
2. **Like a Dragon--Overwhelming, Flood-like Attack**
3. **Like an Adder--Quick, Fast, Sudden, Deceptive and Unexpected.**

He attacks using 5 Weapons:
1. **Temptations** James 1:12 (Remember, James 1:13 tells us God is *not* the tempter, Satan is.)
2. **Tests** James 1:13 Word tempted also means tested.
3. **Trials** James 1:2, 1 Peter 4:12
4. **Cares of this World** (Mark 4:19)
5. **The S.H.A.Q. Attack** (2 Chron.32:1-18, See in depth explanation at our website: thewarriorsagenda.com)

As a Born Again Spirit Filled Believer, You Have 3 Ways That You Can Respond:

1. **Like a Lion—Bold, with Aggressive Counter Attacks**
2. Like a Lamb—Lay there and be *eaten*. I Peter 5:8
3. Like a Warrior--*Tactically, Strategically, Unexpectedly,Jer.51:20,I Tim 6:12, Eph. 6:13,14*

It's almost...

Chapter 1: Like Spiritual Kung Fu...

In the martial arts there is a particular style of *Kung Fu* known as **Wing Chung** that was created by a *woman* (you go ladies!).

This particular style of Chinese self-defense is one of the fastest, if not **the** fastest style in the world rivaled for speed by only a few others, among them Bruce Lee's, Jeet Kune Do Style. Wing Chung was the original foundation for Bruce Lee that he built his own Jeet-Kune-Do Kung Fu style upon.

Women are very compassionate, considerate creatures and so, true to form, this particular young woman, to make it easier on her students to remember and also make the body easier to defend, divided the body up into three parts.

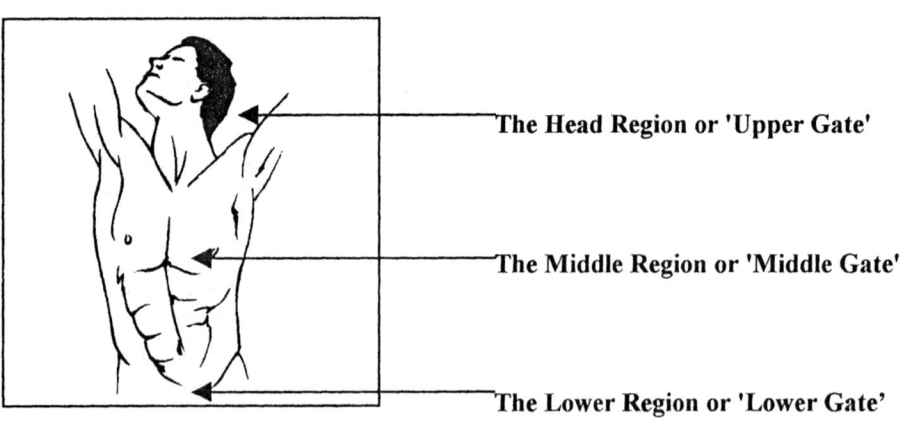

- The Head Region or 'Upper Gate'
- The Middle Region or 'Middle Gate'
- The Lower Region or 'Lower Gate'

Components of the Head Region -- From the Head to the Shoulders.

Components of the Middle Region -- From the Shoulders to the Waist.

Components of the Lower Region -- From the Waist down.

Spiritually speaking for us:

The **'Head'** equates to man's **Mind, which includes his Will, Intellect and Emotions.**

The **'Middle'** equates to man's **Heart, the 'spirit of the human being'.** The *heart* of something always being the 'core'. The core or 'heart' of man, being his ***spirit,*** or ***inner man.*** (Romans 7:22, 2 Cor. 4:16, KJV)

Lastly the **'Lower Part'** representing man's lower nature, i.e. his **Body.** The lower part of the body contains the reproductive organs. Satan, when he launches his attacks to each area, seeks to penetrate our (spiritual) defenses and do mental/emotional, spiritual, and/or physical damage or harm.

When striking 'low' attacking the Body, he seeks to either damage it, by pain, sickness and disease **or** stir within it illicit cravings, unclean habits, lust, addictions, obsessions, uncontrollable desires, etc.

When he attacks the **Middle** area he's going after your **'heart', your inner man or human spirit.** Seeking to impact it with Fear, Doubt, Unbelief, Bitterness.

And when he attacks the **Upper Gate, your Mind,** it's to strike through and 'damage' you mentally with Envy, Confusion, Anxiety, Worry, Depression, jarring imaginations and other negative things.

He is aware that, if you allow him to, he can access and attack your spirit man directly or by going through your other Gates to attack your Spirit Man. Why? Because both your **Body,** the **Lower** Gate, and your **Mind,** the **Upper** Gate are '*Gate-Ways*' to your Spirit Man. If you *think* on a Fear long enough, it will get into your heart—Spirit Man (...As a man **THINKETH**, in his *heart*, so **IS** he. Prov. 23:7) Or, if you allow your **Body** to meditate on and crave a particular *sin* long enough, it will want to *do* it, dragging you right along with it, afterwards leaving your Spirit Man feeling dirty, ashamed, guilty and sinful. That's why Paul said "I keep under my Body (I keep it under control) and bring it into subjection lest... I myself should be a castaway."

Your spiritual defenses then must be designed, as in Kung Fu, to effectively cover all three areas of your being. You must be prepared to _'block' and counter-strike_ _just as in a real fight_. Because, guess what? This **IS** a **real fight**. Just as real as anything you would encounter on the street, because Satan fully intends, if you let him, to knock you out and take what's yours; life, health, strength, family, finances, home, your dreams, your call, etc.

Below, you will see the spiritual and martial art equivalents.

Satan attacks no different than a mugger, robber, or aggressor on the street.

Why is that? Because, whether they know it or not, or admit it or not, when they rob and kill and steal, they are working for him. (John 10:10, John 8:44) He's their *spiritual father*--and again, like father, like son!

Example: When you are having a problem focusing your thoughts, you seem dazed and confused for no reason at all that you can think of, and it's been going on for a while.

That is a *Head Strike*. Satan is attacking your **Mind.**

Or, you're scared of what may happen with your rent, job, business, career, marriage or relationships. Fear seems to *haunt* you, dogging your steps. You can't sleep at night. Or you may actually see or hear things moving in your house or room at night. That's all designed to frighten you, terrify you. Fear is actually a *spirit*, and that *spirit* uses and releases '**fear**' as a 'weapon' and as a literal negative spiritual *force* against you. That's why you can *feel* it, (when something or someone frightens you unexpectantly, you don't grab your head, you grab your heart—you put your hand on your chest over your heart). Fear, like Faith is a real tangible detectable *Force*. Satan is attacking the core of your being, hitting in the very midst or '**middle**' of you. He's going after your 'heart', looking to impact your Spirit Man, your very *core* of existence. It is the seat of where your Spiritual Power comes from via the Holy Spirit and the Lord Jesus Christ. Because he knows that if he can *plant* fear there, it will grow on it's own, you will perpetuate it and you will be your own worst enemy. Remember the Lord Jesus said that out of your 'belly' shall flow rivers of Living Water? (John 7:38). Satan seeks to *muddy* those waters with Fear...

Now if, on the other hand, you find that your Body aches and pains for no reason, or you hurt your back or side, or arm, etc. Got a cold that won't go away, *or have strong seemingly uncontrollable physical urges that periodically seem to rise at will and overwhelm you,* then Satan has gone for a low strike--he's attacking you through the **Lower Gate—your Body.**

If Satan attacks to the **'Head'**, with negative, wicked, or frightening imaginations, thoughts, words and ideas, then we respond with a '*block*' i.e., a scripture designed to *block his attack* on our *Thought Life, our Minds*--2 Corinth. 10:4-6

5. ".. Casting *down* imaginations and *every high thing* that exhalteth itself against the knowledge of God and bringing into *captivity every thought* to the obedience of Christ..."Speak this aloud—*emphatically.*

If he attacks to the **'Heart'** we respond with the appropriate defense--Psa 112:7&8. You take that scripture and turn it into a *defensive shield* that covers and protects your Heart from attack by personalizing it, speaking it aloud AND **applying** it!

'*I shall **NOT** be afraid of evil tidings: **MY Heart** is fixed trusting in the Lord! MY Heart is established, I shall **NOT** be afraid until I see **MY** desire upon my **ENEMIES** (Satan and his crew!)."*

Do you see that? You must respond with the *appropriate* defense *against* his attack.

In other words, in a street fight you would not block by your *head* if the attacker **punched** at your *stomach*. That same logic is true in *Spiritual* Conflict, i.e., **Spiritual Combat.** You must *apply* the right *defense* against the right *attack* for it to work *effectively*. Make sense? Good.

It works.

But don't think that you can read a verse *one* time, take all of ten seconds to do it, and then think--*I got it!*

No, you don't.

It took you longer than *that* to learn your *phone number!* How in the world are you going to learn the **Word of God** and be able to unleash its awesome power if you spend less than 10 seconds a day studying AND applying it?

It's not enough to just **know** it, you must know it, **study it**, and **apply what you know** or it will do you no good. Remember this: It is *not* what you know *about* God's Word that will work for you, but what you act on--**apply** *from it-that will work consistently for you!*

James 1:22. Read it.

If the enemy goes for a 'Low' punch to the 'Body' you respond with a 'low block', a scripture designed to help you keep your Body in check, like Rom. 13:14 *"I make **no provision** for my flesh—I give my flesh no **opportunity** to sin, devil! I don't go where I'm not supposed to go, don't look at what I'm not supposed to see, nor do what I am not supposed to do, nor do I linger around those who do these things! Now shut up flesh and get in line, we're going home! Seeya devil! Have fun playing with your**self**, cause **I'm outta here!**"* And 1 Corinth 9:23-25, if he's endeavoring to manipulate your flesh to cause you to sin. Or, you can use aggressive scripture references regarding healing, if he's attacking your body with sickness.

These references that I have given are just a few, there are scores more, but **YOU** must find them and dig them out for yourself. As you do, you'll find maybe 5 or more scriptures (there are plenty more) per area. But group them in small bite-size portions, then start to study them, read them, meditate them, ***internalize*** them. Shortly you will notice that several will really stand out to you, minister to your heart, create a spark inside.

Those are the one's you need to memorize, personalize and ***apply***. They will work for you powerfully and effectively. Then move on to the next group to cover the next area.

"Wow Brother Humphrey, that sure seems like it could take a lot of time to do and study!"

Yeah, but not as much time as you spent in the hospital the last time you went. Nor as much time as you spent worrying about going to court, or about your son or daughter, or that last time you spent rolling around on the floor in pain.

We have *got* to wake up folks. We've been lazy. The Word of God is like the old 'Mr. Goodwrench commercial'.

Pay me <u>now</u> or pay me later.

You either study the Word of God NOW...*or later*, in the hospital, or bankruptcy court, or divorce court, or the unemployment line or the prescription counter, *after* Satan and his crew have kicked your butt.

I know. I've been there.

It's your choice.

Study now, or study later—in pain and under duress. What's it gonna be?

Again, the choice is yours.

Let's make the right choice...

Chapter 2 Battle Tips:
Spiritual Boxing...

When the enemy feels that he has you where he wants you—on the ropes, defeated, or *feeling* defeated, depressed, hopeless, confused, isolated, disillusioned, doubtful, or fearful, etc., he will lay it on pretty thick, blow after blow.

This is designed to take you down and to take you out, to convince you to give up and surrender to him. If you're in a situation where he makes it quite evident it is *him*, i.e., whatever spirit is attacking you does so boldly, openly, not applying the usual tactic of 'hiding' behind circumstances, but is almost 'bragging' so to speak, this could be typified as a **Lion Style Attack**. Bold, aggressive, out front and in the open. As we explained on page 5, this is the *first* of the three main ways he likes to attack.

If the attack appears to be overwhelming, and you feel like a tennis ball being smacked back and forth across a net, tossed around in the wind and being swept along like a leaf on the ground, odds are then this is the **Dragon Style Attack.**

On the other hand, if you're hit by different types of unusual circumstances, repeatedly, one after the other, family, friends, job, car, home, business, health, appliances, etc., all sudden, quick, and unexpected. Nothing really blatant that says it's the enemy per se—but *you* know who it is. You recognized the technique. Then he's attacking like a *serpent* in the grass, an **Adder Style Attack.** And if you seem to be facing ALL three at once, *that* is a **S.H.A.Q. Attack.**

Now, a good boxer, fighter, Martial Artist, or Warrior, if he or she gets hit and dazed, will slip and dodge blows, but will always at the same time put themselves in a position to throw **counter-punches** that will have a telling effect upon their adversary.

You must do the same thing.

A good fighter always quickly and accurately discerns the 'angle' of attack. Which direction did the attack come from?

In other words, when Satan or his cronies attack you, what exactly are they going after?

Head?

Heart?

Body?

OR are they not going after you per se, but what you *own* and are responsible for, your property/house, car, finances, job, career, income, business, ministry?

OR something more personal, your marriage, your family, your reputation, dear friend, church member, Pastor, loved one?

This type of assessment must be done quickly and accurately. Once an attack is launched, it should be responded to, powerfully, effectively and immediately.

Another important point too is that not only must a boxer quickly discern where the punch is coming *from*; he must discern just as quickly where the punch is *NOT* coming from.

Many Christians erroneously think that it is the Lord 'beating' and 'punching' on them.

Any professional fighter in the middle of a heavy weight championship bout who turned to his corner and said to his manager and to his trainer "Why are you guys *hitting* me?" would immediately be considered too *punch drunk* and beat up to continue!

He would also immediately get knocked out as soon as he turned around *placing his back to his opponent!*

To see a boxer do that in a real fight would seem silly, wouldn't it? Yet, **we** are in a *real fight* and many Christians unfortunately and without knowing it, do that exact same thing, and consequently are *'knocked out'*. Indeed, knocked out spiritually, financially, mentally, emotionally, etc...

They turn around in the middle of a punishing fight with Satan and say to **the Lord, *their trainer*,** and to **the Father, *their Manager*,**

"Why are You doing this to me? Why are You beating on me like this? Why are you making my life so hard?"

And before the Lord can answer and say: **"It's not Us! It's him, the devil, now turn around and figh—"**

Whamm! Fights over and the announcer says:

"Winnerrrrr by knock out and newww Champion in the Life of this Un-informed Christian, Satannnnn!"

Satan has knocked them on their behinds and our loving Father God and the Lord Jesus Christ have gotten the blame...

Then, the Christian rolls over on his or her back, still groggy and says,

"I don't know why the Lord did this to me," or "I don't know why the Lord let this happen to **me**.."

He didn't. He tried to warn us, but we were so busy looking in the *wrong direction* we got ourselves out of position and knocked out, and since we were looking at the Lord when it happened, and were scripturally ignorant (Hosea 4:6), we thought **the Lord** did it to us!

And of course Satan helped to perpetuate that lie.

How? He says one of the following three things

A. God did it.

B. God *told me* to do it.

C. God was trying to teach you something.

Why would he say that?

Because,

A. He thinks we'll be stupid enough to believe it.

B. He knows if we think God sent him, *we won't fight back*.

C. He knows that if we knew the *truth* we'd take the Word of God and knock *him* out, and that the Lord would **bless us** for doing it! Prov. 25:21-22. (Bread in this verse equals the Word. Water mentioned here also equals the Word. I think you can figure out who 'the enemy' is...*Hmmm*?)

(You've got to understand folks; the Lord and the Devil *don't like* one another. They aren't pretending. They actually **ARE** enemies you know...Psa 94:20, Heb. 2:14 KJV)

A good boxer when he's hit, does not stand still and *take* further punishment. He slips away, punching as he moves, **hard punishing blows**, never indicating verbally, physically or with his eyes or movements to his opponent that he is hurt.(Jer.12:5) If the other guy finds out he's going to have to figure it out on his own, because a smart boxer is *not* going to tell him.

Most boxers (90%), even the ones who are losers, have been in better *shape* for their 'matches' than we have as Christians for ours. This should not be the case.

We as Christians should be precise in everything we do. In the way we move, spiritually, mentally, and physically.

Smooth and prepared in the way we think and respond to the enemy's attacks. We should respond quickly and automatically because we are ready and have practiced and are prepared. We should eventually respond without having to stop and think about it. We should be so full of **God's Word** that we have responded before we even realized it. Devastating Satan so quickly with it, and to such a degree, he must withdraw and ponder what to do next. Just like the Lord Jesus did to him. Luke 4:13. (See Amplified Bible)

Don't fight with other Christians, your Pastor, your family, your spouse, your friends, nosey relatives, backbiting people, church members, the trash man, mailman, pet goldfish, your boss, or even *yourself*. None of the above are your enemies. Simply because someone may get on your nerves sometimes, does *not* make them your enemy. You get on their nerves too!

But we all have <u>one</u> *common* enemy, an enemy by the way, who has already been **defeated**. But do you know what?

He's forgetful.

And he needs to be **reminded** on a regular basis.

So that **defeat** just has to be *reapplied* sometimes in order to get his *attention* and remind him that we *know* he's defeated. And then he and his cronies will back away from you for a while, a 'season'. Lk 4:13.

Remember that.

He is *already* a defeated foe who must be **reminded with a good butt whipping from the Word of God** every now and then that *he* is **not** in charge of our lives...

Next, don't expend valuable spiritual energy on things that are counter-productive; jealousy, envy, strife, sin, backbiting and other things that don't aid you in your spiritual development.

Why?

Because, Satan and his crew are very precise and cunning in combat. The victory is yours if applied correctly, but if not, you let the devil win or knock you out on a 'technicality'.

Remember what Paul said,

1 Corinthians 9:25-27 Amplified, (*the Dave Humphrey Version*, but it'll hold water)

26...I do not box as one beating the air (*swinging and missing—eyes closed, getting hit but not knowing where the blows are coming from and flailing just hoping to hit something*).

Striking without an adversary...(*the adversary either having struck and is now long gone, or the adversary having stepped back out of range of my wild blows*).

25... Now every athlete who "goes into training"

(This shows that we too should most definitely go into training, in the Word, Speaking it at the enemy and Praying it to the Father. Remember, you SPEAK the Word to the Enemy, but you PRAY the Word to The Father!) conducts himself temperately and restricts himself in all things. They do it to obtain a wreath that withers, But we do it (i.e., train and discipline ourselves) to obtain an Eternal Crown of Blessedness!"

Train...

Auto Response

Martial Artists train to be *reflexive*--to respond to an attack quickly and automatically without having to stop and think about it. This eliminates confusion, doubt, anxiety, and hesitation. Always remember this:

Hesitation in *any* self-defense situation provides an attacker both time and *incentive* to attack you...

Like Kung Fu, your responses must be automatic.
Prepare in advance for Satan's attack. Eph. 6:12-13 Amplified
Take scripture and *build* it into yourself!
So that when the 'Adder' strikes, you can respond automatically with a spiritual 'punch' or 'kick'.
If two guys attacked your wife, child, or loved one physically, you'd respond with kicks and punches.
Spiritually, have you trained your*self to respond from the heart with God's Word, in* Power?
Practice and build NOW, while there's no pressure.
The U.S. trains hard in *peacetime* so that when there is a war they are *ready* to respond, and NOT trying to figure out what to do. We had that happen

once regarding our Navy. December 7th, 1941, Pearl Harbor, and then again with the Twin Towers.

We have to train *ourselves* so that our response will be immediate--and with the appropriate scripture.

Doubt- Psa 112:7 & 8

Sickness- Isa.53:4,5, Gal.3:13&14, I Peter 2:24, Matt. 8:16&17

Fear - 2 Tim 1:7

Do it *NOW*.

Chapter 3
Skill Builders

In the Martial Arts there are various skill development techniques that we can adapt for our Warfare to improve our "Spiritual Self-Defense Techniques".

Meditate in the Word of God; this is the equivalent of doing sit-ups in the Martial Arts.

What's the point?

Sit-ups *tighten* flabby stomach muscles, true. But they also **toughen your stomach muscles** so that if a punch slips through and hits you every now and then, you don't collapse and fold up in pain.

Benefit: *Meditation in the Word grounds you, puts the Word deep into your Heart, your* **Spirit Man** *and* **"Toughens you"** *so that you're able to stand the enemy's* **punch** *if one slips through. You won't double over in the spiritual 'pain' of doubt, fear, or worry.*

Sparring

Another technique used to train beginning martial artists is called:

One Step Sparring: This is designed to carefully and gradually build up your knowledge of some basic and specific self defense techniques by allowing you and your partner to start out practicing them slowly until you gradually have increased your knowledge, improved your speed and progress to 'free sparring'—an all out application of what you have learned in a fast action setting closer to real life.

Is this applicable for the Christian?

Yes.

Speak r Word un purpose! w/ authority

Partner with someone that is close to you and a committed Christian who knows the Word. Or at least find someone who is willing to work with you and follow your requests.

Have them *test* you regularly (minimum weekly) on your knowledge of the Word and how **prepared** you are to *use* it when life's circumstances and Satan attacks.

Have them challenge you. For example, here's an easy one.

Partner: *"Satan attacks your finances with an unexpected $1250.00 bill. What do you do, how do you respond."*

Then, **your job** is to respond with the appropriate 'Scripture Block and Punch' combination.

You: *"No weapon that is formed against me shall prosper! Not even financial weapons! Isa 54:17* (That's your 'block'. If fired from your mouth and Heart, in Faith and Power, it 'Blocks' Satan's attack.) *MY GOD shall supply all my need according to His riches in glory by Christ Jesus!* (That's your **Attack Scripture**, your **counter-punch**. Or if you wanted to be even *more* aggressive you could use Psalm 35:6, *also*).

Understand?

Active, aggressive, *application* of **The Word**.

This is what the Lord did in Matt.4 and Luke 4.

Tell your partner to *not* let you off the hook by allowing you to say, "Uhh, well, umm, I uh.. Would uhh, pray about it."

We're not covering prayer yet. **This is SPEAKING the Word.** *Something the Lord Jesus did, DAILY, or whenever the enemy showed up! This should not be a lost art among us as Christians today.*

When you stand on Word all heaven is working w/you

Now this same technique of knowing the Word, where it's found, and being able to speak it freely, with no—'umms', or 'uhhs', or 'I think it's..' or some such excuse, is **vital**.

We **have** to know the Word. That's <u>**our responsibility.**</u>

The Lord is not going to do that part *for* us.

He's not going to *learn it* for us. He already *knows* it, so we have to *too*! Josh. 1:8.

When you speak it on purpose, practicing it with another Believer as we've shown you above, **now**, in 'peace-time', this is a form of spiritual ***'Sparring'***.

Practice this in each area of your health, finances, mental health, home, job, etc. There is a Word or Promise of God in the Bible to cover *every* situation we are confronted with.

The Lord has given us these Scriptures to *use* them.

It's **our** job to study them, learn them, practice them and *apply* them.

Benefit: When Satan comes you will be prepared and ready in those areas you have read, meditated, studied and 'sparred' in. He will be unable to frighten you and catch you off guard. You will recover from any surprise attack more quickly. You will not break and run from sudden fear. You will hold your ground. You will catch *him* by surprise for a change. The Angels of God will hold ground with you (Psa. 103:20,) fight for you and with you, (Psa 35:5&6) more readily.

Seems just a little 'too practical', mechanical?
It's not.
Our Father is practical, that's why He gave us 'two' legs to get around on instead of just *one*!
Find it too mechanical to practice meditating, memorizing, then speaking the Word like that?
Tell it to our Father. But I don't think you'll get very far though. It was **His** idea in the first place! Josh. 1:8 (Read it).
Now, get to work with your partner and let's *Spar*.
Remember, Spiritually, always keep your guard up.

Sit Ups

Reading the Word of God is like 'Jogging', but **meditation** in the Word of God is like doing **Sit Ups**, it helps you to 'toughen' yourself spiritually for the battles to come. As you meditate in the Word of God you help *build* it deep down in your spirit, your inner man. And just like sit ups do for a boxer, when the enemy starts punching, if a few blows slip through, you're tough enough to absorb it and keep on going and punch back, counting it all joy. James 1:2-4.

Meditation helps the Word of God go from just your *head* down to your *spirit*. That's vital; here's why.

Punching

It is an interesting fact that the better shape your stomach muscles are in, they actually assist you to a certain degree in providing more power to your punches. The other thing one is taught in the art of Kung Fu is to never 'punch just using the shoulder', but rather using the whole body. In other words, **put all of your body weight behind the blow.**

Bruce Lee was phenomenally good at this and demonstrated this once by placing his fist only **one inch** away from a volunteer's stomach. In one minor flex of his fist, he then generated enough power to send this 6' 2" tall, over 200 pound Black Belt, flying backwards and into a chair placed 6 feet away behind the man! The over 2500 people who saw the live demonstration were stunned.

What's the point?

The point is this, *we* as believers have to discover and realize that power is not generated from your *head* when you speak the Word of God at the enemy, but from your **spirit**. *Meditation* in the Word and Praying in the Spirit **help to 'build' that power (Jude 20), and 'speaking' the Word <u>releases</u> it**(Ecc 8;4,Job 22:28).

A punch done just using the shoulder muscles is no where near as effective or damaging as putting your *whole body behind it*. Shoulder strength is say 20-30 lbs for the average person, vs. *160 lbs*, (or however much you weigh), put solidly behind your punch.

The same is true with the **Word of God.** The Power of releasing it comes from within the core of your being, your *spirit man*, the *very heart* of you, where the Holy Spirit resides.

Think about it.

Most Christians don't speak the Word of God from their **Heart**, but from their <u>Head</u>.

"Boy I sure hope this works! Man oh man, I know it's the Word of God, **but...**" And then they wonder why it doesn't work.

The last time you were on the phone and your little Johnny, or little Mary, or Keisha were making such a racket that you couldn't hear, you said;

"Stop Keisha, mommy is on the phone and can't hear, you're making too much noise."

Then, you went back to talking on the phone...and *they went back to making noise.*

"Stop now, I said, mommy can't hear," you repeated.

Ten minutes later they're still going—in fact, they got *louder.* Then, *you* said:

"Girlllllll! You better stop that noise and you better stop it right NOW, or your behind is MINE!!! You hear me!!"

After that, it was like the *Night Before Christmas,* because all through the house, not creature was stirring, not even a *mouse!* They shut up fast!

Why?

Because the first time you said it, you would have '*liked*' for them to have stopped what they were doing. But, that *last* time you said it, you **meant** for them to stop it and stop <u>right then</u>—*or else!* That's the **exact** same way you have to do the devil and his demons.

The first two times came from your 'head'. The last time came from your <u>**heart**</u>*!*

Nothing that you have ever said from just your *head* has ever changed anything.

But! Everything that you have ever said *from the bottom of your heart* has changed your *life—forever.*

I'm sure you can think of some examples, both good *and* bad...

It works, and in the area of speaking the Word at the enemy, that's *how* it works, and why.

So, to say it once again, <u>Meditation in the Word builds the capacity within you to not just speak it from your head, but your *heart*</u>.

It's like eating. You chew your food first and then swallow it. In other words, it is transferred from your mouth to your stomach for digestion and distribution to the body for strength and energy.

As you **meditate the Word**, the mind 'breaks it up' into bit size pieces, releasing the inherent *spiritual nutrients* therein. It then 'transfers' them down into your spirit man (like swallowing) where the spiritual nutrients of power, faith, love, compassion, and an accurate perception of God's Will along with spiritual strength, are all distributed through out your "spiritual system" providing spiritual strength and energy for the fight and God's service.

Make sense?

But Brother Humphrey, what about praise, and worship, and fellowship with the Father?

You should *already* be doing that. That is a given. Listen to me carefully...

We are not here to study what you **already know** about Spiritual Combat. We're here to study what you **don't**.

You should already know how to deal with the Father in praise and worship and fellowship, we've been learning that for years, thank God.

But what most Christians **don't know** is how to deal with the **enemy** effectively, and that's what we are here to examine. Always remember this:

Reading the Word, provides **Information**.

Studying the Word, provides **Facts**.

Mediation in the Word, provides *Revelation*.

We need to do all three--daily.

Chapter 4
Only Forward—Never Back

Some styles of martial arts teach that one should never retreat in the face of the enemy, but rather turn and *evade* incoming blows, by turning the body sideways and deflecting them.

Going back to our example of Wing Chung, one is taught to turn to the side and deflect the oncoming force of an aggressor rather than to give ground.

How is that relative to *Spiritual Combat*?

A lot of times we as believers can unwittingly 'give ground' to the enemy. He is a natural *aggressor* who will take every inch of ground in our lives that we give him. You should never have to shed tears or blood for the same ground twice.

What do I mean?

We'll examine two areas in which Satan endeavors to make a believer retreat so that he can 'gain ground'—they are *healing* and *finances*.

The first time you learned about God's Covenant promise regarding your healing, and that the Lord Jesus bought and paid for that for you (Isa. 53:4&5, I Peter 2:24, Matt 8:16&17) you were thrilled and amazed at such an awesome and loving God! Remember?

You were absolutely delighted the very first time the Lord healed you through the Word or in answer to prayer.

The first time you got a headache or body ache or pain or dizziness, etc. after that discovery, you jumped on it with both feet and a hefty dose of the Word of God. You wouldn't budge, not one inch. You told the devil to stop.

That you *didn't have time for him and his conniving ways any more* and to beat it!

Now, after several years, when a pain hits, what do you do? Grab for your Bible, OR do you grab for the Ben Gay, Tylenol or Icy Hot?

See what I mean?

No, this is not to condemn you. I've been there too. And there's no prohibition in the Word against using medicine, and no, using medicine is not a sin. As Father's children, He wants us to grow spiritually in the *effective application of His Word* to our lives so that eventually we stay healed and we won't *need* it. So that no sickness, pain or disease will be able to cling like lint to our bodies. But the problem is that we have 'retreated' somewhere down the line and the enemy moved in and set up stakes. Little, by little, inch by inch.

How?

The first few times that headache came we use to beat it off with the Word of God.

"How dare you touch me devil! I'm **God's** property! **Get outta here!**"

He leaves.

A month or two later, he comes back.

"*Hmmm maybe now he or she is not **reading, and studying** as much as they were before. Not **meditating** in the Word as much. Let's try it now.*" **{Luke 4:13 Amp}**

You feel a pain or discomfort.

"Ouch! Devil I told you last month—beat it! In the Name of Jesus!"

He leaves again.

Waits a little while...

In the *mean time* God has blessed. We got a raise, things are going well.

With the new raise or new job comes new responsibilities. **{Prov. 14:4 *Always be aware that with the greater blessing, always comes the greater responsibility. Where no oxen are, the crib is 'clean'—there's no ox 'poop' to clean up. But with more 'oxen' comes the ability to do more, and be blessed more—but there also comes more 'ox poop' to clean up too—more work and responsibility!*}** New responsibilities means more time usually spent at work. More time at work means less time for self. Less time for self, means less time to do what you want. Less time to do what you want means less time to read. Less time to read, means less time in the Word...

Starting to see the pattern?

Satan returns.

So does the pain.

You rebuke it, but...

It doesn't go away *as quickly* as it did the other times. It starts to linger. You rebuke again.

"I *know* by Jesus' stripes I am healed!"

And according to the Word, which is THE Truth—you are.

Ah, but the problem is you don't *feel* like it, do you. The pain lingers. You've rebuked, you've resisted, you've prayed. Nothing happened (not at least that you could see).

You wonder why, unaware that your Word level has *dropped* dramatically. You use to spend much more time reading and meditating in the Word. Now, because of time constraints, it's just ten minutes.

Got to hurry to work, can't be late, God's blessed us so we bought a house or moved to a better apartment. Ah, but now the commute is *farther*, gotta get the kids off to school earlier, etc.

Hurry, hurry, hurry!

Whether married or single, think back. How much time do you spend in the Word *now*, compared to what you *use* to? Starting to see some things clearer now?

But Brother Humphrey, I do my praise and worship every day with the Lord!

That's good! Excellent! But you know what?

A plant does not just need '*sunshine*' to grow, but **'water'** too. He is the vine, but *you* are the branch {John 15:5} and *you* need sunshine **and** the 'water' of the Word—daily.{Eph. 5:26, **Make sure you turn to this scripture and read it. You need to *know* what it says.**}

If the Word was not vital for our daily living, the Lord would not have likened it to "Bread" {Luke 4:4} But now, back to our examples...

So, the pain lingers even after we've 'rebuked' it.

We know we've been away from the Word, but we say:

"Lord, I'm late for work! I ain't got time for this now! I got to be there in *10 minutes*! And I got a meeting this morning too!

"And Lord you know all those projects I *have* to get done that were due yesterday! You *told me* to start on them last week, I should have *listened* to You! Now I've **got** to get them done!"

" And Lord you **know** what kind of boss I have!

"And I'm sorry, I know I should've been studying your Word last night, but my *show* came on last night

And I missed it last week so you know I just *had* to see it..."

"And after that I was *soooo* tired, that I just fell asleep!"

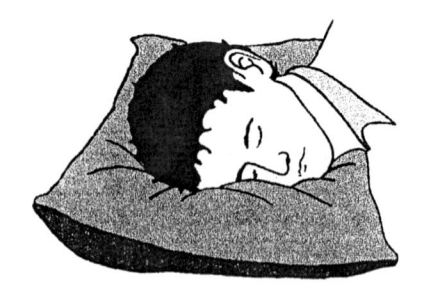

"When I get home this evening though, I'm gonna study **real good**. I promise..."

And of course, we usually never do, because something *else* comes up.

Satan has just moved inside the borders of your "healing territory" and set up camp, an outpost.**{Eph. 4:27 The greek word used in this passage is the basis for our english word 'topography—the study of maps'. So what's the Holy Spirit saying? Don't give the devil any 'land' or 'ground' in your life. It is a military term. No retreat—no surrender. Nail that invader when you see him first stick a foot on your territory to test your 'resistance'.}** This pain was a 'cross border raid', from his territory to yours to see what *you* would do about it. *Not* what *the Lord* would do about it—but *you*! The Lord has *already* done something about it. He died and gave His healing to *you*. What Satan wants to see is what are *you* going to do about it and are you willing to **fight** to *keep* it! Always remember this. Where Satan gets no strong spiritual resistance from you using the Word and prayer, he sets up camp. First an **'outpost'** (occasional pain or minor but persistent ailment), then a **'camp'** (unusual condition, mysterious lump that won't go away, or, condition that comes and goes) and finally a full and complete **Base of Operations** (cancer, heart condition, high blood pressure, arthritis, etc) from which he then operates to attack other areas of your life and body, including your mind (a head strike to the upper gate) with worry. *What is* ***this****? How come it's not going away? Wonder what it is?*

Understand?

Now it's time for our next example:

Finances.

He attacks your money. You use to viciously respond from the Word, with scriptures regarding the meeting of your financial needs. He attacked you, then, when you would attack back:

WHAM!

You'd receive money in ways you never thought of. People gave you money, you got a raise or better job, you found money laying in the street(a personal frined of mine several years ago prayed earnestly because he was $200 short on his rent. Afterwards while walking down the street with another believer on the way to church, they waited to cross at a traffic light. While standing there the Holy Spirit said to him, "Son, look down." There, gently blowing down the gutter was two $100 dollar bills. He nudged the other Christian and said. "You just asked me if the Lord had answered my prayer yet. Look." He bent down and picked up the money, thanked the Lord and they continued on to church rejoicing.)

You found money that you'd forgotten you had, people called you on the phone who *owed* you money and finally started to pay up. It was a blessing. The Angels of God worked *overtime* to meet your needs!

As time went on, you started getting a little resistance in certain areas. The money that was coming in started to slow down a little bit. Payroll started messing up on your check, or your job cut back your hours, etc. Now, instead of finding money you forgot you had, you start finding bill collectors calling to remind you of *bills* that you'd forgot that you had. Things start going wrong with the car, or the fridge, dryer, computer, air conditioning, plumbing or heat, the house.

They cost money to fix.

Seems like things started out well then slowed to a *trickle*. Now you barely have enough to make ends meet, or, at the very least, are starting to feel the 'pinch'. You say, oh, this will pass.

In the mean time Satan's cronies are in your 'financial territory' setting up shop astride your financial 'supply line' to choke off your money.

In this Spiritual fight that you and I are involved in, wherever we 'back up' Satan moves forward—*aggressively*, sometimes subtly, but always constantly, until he is stopped.

None of the above things are said to condemn. Please do not construe them that way. The reason why I can speak to them with such detail is because I've been there.

Now, what do we do about it.

Fight.

Get back in the Word and do your spiritual 'push ups'. Get back in the Word and train. 'Spar' with a trusted spiritual partner who will hold you accountable to learn what you once knew, again.

Yeah, I know. Some of those scriptures that you knew, you still remember and have been quoting them. Maybe you've never stopped, but yet you note that it's still not working.

Why?

A primary reason could be what we mentioned before. You're saying them from your 'head' and not your spirit—your *heart*. That's where the **power** comes from. That's where the Holy Spirit resides. He is the Power within you. Not yourself.

It's like one of those chocolate Easter bunnies you use to get as a kid. You've got the 'chocolate shell' on the outside, i.e. you can still *quote* it, but you haven't spent any time lately **'meditating'** <u>in</u> it so that the Holy Spirit can fill you with the 'substance' of that verse again, not just the 'wording' of it. Chocolate bunnies are good, but not quite as good as they are with the 'filling' inside!

In the martial arts one is taught to 'punch from the hip' with your whole body behind it, that's where the power comes from. The Word and the Holy Spirit teach: meditate in the scriptures and punch from the 'heart'—the spirit man; that's where the **REAL power** comes from. Why?

Because that's where the Word is, that's where the Holy Spirit is if you're born again, and the Holy Spirit **always** acts on the Word of God, and *backs* it.

He *makes* it HAPPPEN! {Gen. 1:2&3 Notice that in verse 2 the Mighty Holy Spirit of God was *moving*, but nothing was happening. Nothing happened *until* Father Spoke His Word (vs 3) and then—BANG! There was light.

Why? Because the Holy Spirit *ALWAYS acts upon the Word of God*. God bless our churches, all of them that are founded upon the Lord and His Word. But this is why in a lot of cases there has been no great explosion of His Presence. We have the Holy Spirit *moving* in our churches, but nothing really happening. Praise God, yes, people get touched. Yes, people get *blessed*. But in the *New Testament* every time the Holy Spirit moved—BANG! *Something* happened! People got healed, blind eyes were opened, folks were raised from the dead and consequently, sinners flooded the church!

[This last incident happened again recently in Africa, Praise God.

While an Evangelist was up preaching the Word as the Spirit was *moving*, a woman had brought her dead husband to the service because just before he had died, he made his wife promise she would. The ushers wouldn't allow her to bring the body into the service. Understandably afraid that it would freak people out. Hmph. Can't help but wonder though if they felt that way in the early church?

Anyway, she insisted and they said no, but that she could take it in the basement, in a room *under* the the main sanctuary and that happened to be directly under the pulpit. While Rhinehart Bonnke, the evangelist, preached upstairs, the man started breathing and came back to life. And then sat up, then spoke. By the way, this was AFTER the man had already been *embalmed*. Don't believe it? Believe it. I've seen the video. The doctor who pronounced him dead and the mortician who did the embalming we amazed and astounded and after 'meeting' the man declared emphatically that it had to be a miracle. Man! Why does all the good stuff happen in Africa! Because they believe God and take Him seriously at His Word. Rhinehart always has a film crew with him to record the crowds that come to his meeting. People wouldn't believe it otherwise because in Africa he draws crowds of 200,000 to 1 million. Yes, you read that correctly. 1 million. Why? Because of the miracles and because of the Word.

This was the calling card of God through out the early church. No one else could match the power of what Our Heavenly Father did through the Christians, not even the demon possessed magicians. *THAT's* why Christianity grew so fast. The people saw the miracles, then heard the Word, and got saved. Father was *not* the one who wanted to stop doing miracles, it's just that **we as** a church *stopped believing Him for them.* Satan 'camped' in that area of unbelief and has been trying to stay there ever since.

The Holy Spirit confirmed the Word with signs following and the church grew in an explosion of souls because people saw the Truth with *proof*! Mk 16:20, Acts 2:41, Acts 4:4, Acts 5;14. I Cor.2:4&5.

Today instead we have 'programs'. I understand one brother started doing his sermons with a 'ventriloquist's dummy' to help him. No, he wasn't a youth pastor. I could understand doing it for the kids, but he was using the dummy with the *adults* in the morning service... To make his sermons more *'interesting'* and entertaining.

Amazing.

We've gone from the Power of God, to 'Puppets' in the pulpit. Lord help us...

In contrast, in the New Testament Church, *this* was the process: A man or woman of God filled with the Word, Speaks it/Prays it out. The Holy Spirit manifests, moves upon His people and acts upon the Word attesting to the Lordship of Jesus and glorifying Him through confirming of the Word of God. Sinners see and are drawn by the wonders and undeniable miracles. They receive the Word preached to them because their hearts are open and they are eager to hear. They hear the Word and get saved. The wonders *don't* save them. The Word does that, but Father and the Holy Spirit *use* the signs and wonders to meet the needs of saint and sinner alike and confirm to a skeptical and sin-weary world that *Jesus* and His Word are *true*! {Acts 2:22} Get it? Ok, back to our lesson.) Should we seek the signs *alone*, just for the sake of having them?

No! But like the early church did we should 'earnestly desire the best gifts' of the Holy Spirit because signs and wonders *are* part of the overall manifestation of the Holy Spirit and God's plan.

That's what the early church did from the Word, and Father responded!

While the Holy Spirit was *moving,* the Church in Acts prayed "...By stretching forth your hands to *heal* and that <u>*signs and wonders* maybe done in the **Name of Thy Holy Child Jesus**</u>!" [Acts 4:30]

We generally speak the Word *before* the manifest presence of the Holy Spirit, and *afterwards*, but not during, because we're all usually caught up in the bliss of His Presence. Thank God for it. But we as a whole haven't discovered yet that the Holy Spirit always comes (manifests) Himself for a *reason*.

Infact, the Lord Jesus explained that there were several. Let's examine what He said closely and we will see that there are 3 primary reasons the Holy Spirit comes (manifests).

1. To Testify of Jesus, i.e., confirm that Jesus *is* Lord, by attesting miracles and signs and wonders done in His Name. Mk 9:38, John 15:26. Acts 3:6.

2. To Glorify Him, i.e., through the actions sanctioned by the Lord Jesus that He said were to be done in His Name by the church. John 16:14, John 14:12-14 Acts 3:6, 16, Acts 4:3,7,8,10,12,18. Matt 28:18-20 & Mark 16:15-18 and 20!!! And what was the result: Acts 5:14-16.

3.a) To Minister to the needs of His people, i.e., guide us into all 'truth'. And this is done in a number of ways. He helps us to understand His Word in it's completeness, fullness, because the 'truth' He speaks of here (John 16:14) is the *exact* same truth He speaks of in the *very next* chapter (John 17:17).

b) Makes us aware of what lies ahead, in both our immediate future and our lives as He sees fit, including making us aware of upcoming attempts by the enemy to hinder us, as well as bringing forth prophesy through us via the Gifts of the Spirit Etc, John 16:13. Acts 2:17-18

c) To teach us all things that we need to know to accomplish Father's mission for our lives.

d) To comfort us when we are weary from the battle.

e) Bring all things to our remembrance that He has said unto us, both from the Word and in our personal prayer times with Him. John 14:26

f) Leads us in the things of God and bear witness that we are truly Sons and Daughters of God. Romans 8:14-16.

g) Helps us through our weaknesses and intercedes for us through these times when we may not know what to pray as we should. Rom.8:26 & 27

Chapter 5

The Warrior Mind Set...

There is a very powerful book of action written by a gentleman named David J. Rogers. The title of his book is 'Fighting To Win'.

It is an excellent book on the warrior's 'attitude'

The book unfortunately is no longer in print and the Holy Spirit led me to one of the very *last* copies in, of all places, a 'Salvation **Army**' Store. Someone had donated it and it has impacted my life and the lives of every one the Lord has had me share it with, and it will impact yours too. Let's begin...

The Japanese Samurai were the consumate warriors of their day. One of their maxims was the Japanese phrase **'Makato'**.

We find three terms that every spiritual warrior should be familiar with.

Makato: Putting absolutely everything you *have* and everything you *are* into an act or strike—all of your heart (spirit), mind and physical strength.

Okay… But brother Humphrey what does this have to do with spiritual warfare?

Everything.

The Lord Jesus Christ put it this way,

"The light of the body is the eye: if therefore thine eye be *single*, thy whole body shall be full of light." Matt 6:22.

Do you know what that means?

He's saying to us, among other things to be "single-minded". **Focus** on the thing that needs to be done, or that you're believing God for. **Be** <u>single-minded</u>, **not** *double-minded* (James 1:8).

It is only when you are single-minded that your 'whole body will be full of *light*'.

Meaning?

The Lord will reveal to you *how* to accomplish the thing that you need to get done! Light in the scriptures is used many times to represent revelation, understanding, enlightenment.

It is only when you are **single-minded**, for God, regarding your purpose, your calling, what you're standing on the Word for, what you're seeking God for, or what you are charging the enemy for, that revelation, enlightenment, understanding of <u>**how**</u> to accomplish the thing Father wants done comes to you!

In other words, most people quit and give up before the answer, or the revelation of how to *get* the answer comes.

You have to put everything you have into seeking God. Everything you have into standing on the Word. Everything you have into receiving your answer. Everything you have into crushing the enemy under your feet when he tries to rear up and talk back.

You crush **him**, or he crushes *you*.

He doesn't like being defeated, so, if you let him, he will try to rise and overcome you. You can NOT let him do that. Jesus whipped him, but as the Lord's 'Federal Marshals' deputized with power (Luke 10:19) it's your job and my job to *keep him* down.

'*No, it's not Brother Humphrey that's the Lord's job. The Lord doesn't expect me to do anything about the devil.*"

Then why did the Lord give **His power** to *you*?

"*But the devil's already defeated so it's all over but the Rapture.*"

Again, same question. Then why did God *give His* **Power** to **you**? Luke 10:19, 2 Peter 1:3.

Time for a reality check.

Folks Satan *is* defeated—utterly. But he's not *dead*. So after the Lord whipped him and put him underfoot, the Lord left us here to **keep** Satan underfoot until He returned again.

The Lord is coming back, and the Rapture will be the most glorious thing that we as the Body will experience this side of Heaven next to salvation and the Baptism in the Holy Spirit. But we've all been so eager to go home and be with Jesus, that we forgot that **He** said to "<u>Occupy</u> till I come". Luke 19:13 KJV.

Interesting term the Lord chose to use. In the Greek it means to 'occupy or do business.'

'Occupy' is a military term. Once you conquer an enemy country, you '*occupy it*'. To **suppress** any *additional* rebellion after you have won the war.

But that doesn't mean that the enemy stops shooting even though he's been **beaten.** We found that out in WWI, we found that out in WW II, and we're finding that out again at the time of the writing of this manual, in Iraq.

Pockets of resistance have to be rooted out and crushed.

That's **why** troops 'occupy' an area or country!

That's what **we've** been sent here to do.

'Occupy' and be about our Father's 'business' until the Lord returns.

And do you know what the funny thing is?

As much as we *want* Him to come back, He's already said He's not coming back **UNTIL** this Gospel has been preached in all the earth! Matt. 24:14.

Now, if your boss said that you were not going to get paid *UNTIL* you finished doing your work—*first*. Would you sit around and wait outside of his office whining: "*I sure will be glad when my paycheck comes. Lorrrrrd I'm so tired, I sure could use my paycheck. Wish my pay check would come tomorrow...*"

Now, would you do that, *or* would you go back to your desk and get to **work**?

Payday seems to come real *quick* when you're busy doing your *job*.

Occupy...

Have you ever noticed that in most movies near the end the hero is always *atleast* 20 percent more effective and 20 percent more *aggressive* than he was the first time around? Do you know why? Because some where along the line he's realized that he *has to be* in order to be *successful*!

The same thing is true for you with Satan.

That brings us to our next term, **Mo Chih Chu**. It too is a warrior term the Samurai used. It means *going ahead without hesitation*. For our purposes, it is not looking back *once you have decided on a course of action that the Lord has given you **or** that you have seen plainly given in the Word of God to do*.

It literally means to **leap** into battle without hesitation.

When there was a battle to be fought, the Samurai of ancient Japan always did *two* things.

We must do **three.**

First he drew his sword without delay, then, whether it was against ten men or one, he **leaped** into battle!

The procedure for us, as Christian Warriors should be this; First we **Acknowledge the Lord.** Why? Because of our Battle Orders, Proverbs 3:6: "In all thy ways *acknowledge* Him, and He shall *direct* thy paths!" In other words, acknowledge Him and He will direct your paths, including your path of attack. Notice here that it does **not** say 'Thou shalt pray a lonnnng prayer' at this point. You can if you wish, and usually the average *Christian Soldier* does, but the **Christian Warrior** does not.

"*What! He doesn't pray! But Bro. Humphrey, why not!*"

Because (1) He/she has **already prayed!** And (2) Because there comes a time when you have to act and attack, move forward and not just pray. (Ex. 14:13 Moses said: "Stand still..." The Lord said: "Why criest thou to me (Why are you praying)?? Tell the children of Israel to "*go forward*"!)

The **Christian Warrior** has *already* prayed, they **stay** prayed up, therefore, in a moment of battle he or she doesn't 'hesitate', but draws their Sword and moves *forward*.

The average Christian Soldier waits till *the last minute* to do *everything*. *The Warrior* does not.

I recently read a true account of a group of our soldiers in a fierce battle in Vietnam. They were surrounded. A Lieutenant had a lazy soldier in his squad who *never* kept his weapon clean. Nearly everyone in his squad was wiped out. The only weapon the Lt. had left was the .45 pistol that belonged to the lazy soldier.

Thanks to the lazy soldier, the Lt.'s life depended on a 'dirty gun'. Don't wait till you're faced with a battle, and 'then' *clean your gun*.

Don't wait till you're faced with a battle and *then* try to pray.

You better be prayed *up*.

A **Christian Warrior** is already. So he, or she:

1) Acknowledges God.

2) He or she immediately draws their Sword (Eph.6:18, 2 Corth.6:7 *Amplified Bible!*) and

3) He or she **leaps** into battle! *Mo Chih Chu!* Attacking the sickness, disease, poverty, confusion, depression, fear, worry, thoughts, etc. 20% more **aggressively** than last time. Why? Because the Word teaches we are being changed from 'glory *to* glory' (2 Cor 3:18). That means, for one thing,

you are getting *stronger* and *stronger* in the Lord! That's what He **said**, whether *you* feel like it or not. So act like He knows what He's talking about, *because He does*!

Nowhere in the New Testament do you find the Lord being *passive* with the devil and his demons. Nor does He tell us to be so either.

Proverbs 10:6b **AND** 10:9b says"...but *violence coverth the mouth of the wicked."* In other words being **Spiritually** *Violent and aggressive with the Word of God*, shuts Satan up! (Matt.11:12) In this text the Hebrew word for "violence" also means to be **bold, i.e., very aggressive.** Know this. In the battle you face, a *Logos* Word is as good as a *Rhema* Word. Because a *Logos* Word is generally understood as the *written* Word of God and that's what the Lord used to *crush* the enemy with, and the disciples used to do the miraculous. "...And they went forth, and preached every where, the Lord working with them, and confirming *the* **Word (Logos)** with signs following. Amen(so be it)." Mark 16:20.

We must come to understand and believe the truth that, as we've just seen, signs don't just follow a Rhema Word, but the Logos (written Word) too, when we believe it, and act on it (James 2:26). As it is written:

"But be ye doers of the Word (Logos) and not hearers only, deceiving your ownselves..." James1:22.

Let's use *all* of our Holy Ghost weapons and remember to stay *single minded* on the Lord's Word and to:

Makato: Put everything you have into living for God and Speaking His Word and

Mo Chih Chu: Go forward in what the Lord has told you to do **without hesitation...**

Finally there is **Tomaranu Kokoro**, "A mind that knows no stopping."

Many Christians, after a successful 'Faith Victory', answer to prayer, or victory over a temptation, test or trial, relax, take their armour off and completely let their guard down. They take a 'faith vacation'. They hang up their spiritual guns and put their feet up and congratulate themselves on a successful outcome. While watching from a concealed position and licking his wounds, is the enemy. He then launches an immediate counter-attack while we are spiritually 'max'n and relax'n and we're caught off guard. Some fail, some fall, or even worse...

Ever had that happen to you?

You overcome one situation or temptation only to turn right around and fall prey to another one?

Possibly one that was not as hard as the one you just overcame...

What happened?

All true warriors, generals and military men know, the best time to strike back at an enemy is just after he has had a major victory over you. Why? Because he will be so busy celebrating, the last thing he expects is to be attacked.

Understand this, Satan is utterly defeated, but, he is a *strategist*. When you can't defeat an enemy by sheer force, then you use *guile* and *deception*...

He realizes that he can't beat God by sheer force, so, he works to defeat God's *Children*, *us*, by guile and deception. 2 Cor.2:11.

So what do we do?

Tomaranu Kokoro...

After you have a victory over the enemy, his temptation, test or trail—stay alert. Don't let your mind 'stop'. Don't go to sleep spiritually and stop reading, praying, studying, meditating or speaking the Word. You stay strong, firm, committed and alert and move from one target to the next like a spinning top. It's hard to hit a moving target. Don't go to sleep while you're supposed to be on guard duty. Be ready.

Paul put it this way: "..having done all to **stand, stand therefore** {*'ready to do battle again if necessary'* is the implication here in this verse}having your lions girt about with TRUTH (The Word) and having on the Breastplate of Righteousness..."

In other words: ***Keep your Armour on! Be ready for a counter-attack. Stand strong!*** Eph. 6:13&14. Read it.

There is another Samurai saying which puts it this way:

After Victory, tighten your helmet cords!

This is the end of Part One...

The Warrior's Agenda Combat Study Guide:

Learning How To Be *Combat Effective*

In Spiritual Warfare...

God's Principles of Spiritual Self-Defense:

For Your Home, Your Family, Your Vision, Your Life and Your Ministry...

Part 2

Spiritual Self-Defense...

Spiritual Self-Defense. What does it mean?

This course is designed to teach you what should be some of the most basic tenets of Spiritual Self-Defense for the Christian Warrior.

It is vital as a Christian Warrior that you understand several basic things.

1) It is not what you are *aware* of, or even *know* from the Word of God that works for you. It is what you *apply*, from the Word of God that will work for you. That is, what you apply correctly.

2) Never Give Up. The Lord Jesus Christ is not a quitter. He didn't give up on you, and neither can you give up on *yourself*, NOR the dream, goal, ministry or purpose, God gave you.

3) You must *know* and *apply* the Word of God. Not *tradition*. Traditions are concepts, principles, rules, thoughts and religious ideas passed on from one man to another or one woman to another, or one family to another or one minister to another that are regarded with the same solemnity and reverence as the written Word of God. And that's the problem. They are not equal. Any tradition based on a man's idea, however well intended, that is regarded by you or anyone else as being as binding or as true as God's Word, actually prevents the Word of God from working in your life, especially and particularly in that area. Why? Because it is exactly as the Lord Jesus said.

"Your *traditions* have made the **Word of God** of *none effect.*" Matt15:6, Mk 7:13. Paul again warns us about this in Col.2:8. If you only study the Word through the eyes of someone's *tradition*, then you will be as limited as the one you are following in your vision and understanding of the Word.. If they are color blind to certain things in the Word, (and if you NEVER study the Word on your own) then you will be too in those exact same areas. Why? Because you have limited and confined yourself to the same field of vision that *they* have! They say: "This can't be true, God doesn't heal any more." If *you* never study the Word for yourself then you will parrot that.

"God doesn't heal or do miracles any more. That's stopped, that's passed away.

How do you know?

Cause, Bro So and So said so. This is God testing me in this area, He gave me cancer, troubles, bankruptcy, headaches, calamity, car accidents, car trouble, bills, etc, etc, etc.

How do you know?

Cause I told you, *Bro So and So said so!*"

If you can only quote "Bro So and So" and never be able to say: I know the things I believe are true because the *Word says so*, and here is the reference where it's found, then check your stance very carefully because odds are you're standing on *tradition*, not **the Word**. And remember, we are *New Covenant* believers and that's what we live by, what we stand on and what we fight with.

We said in point one that it is not enough to just know the Word of God. While this is true, we are not discounting the importance of knowing the Word of God, merely pointing out that you cannot *stop* there. This is a *stage* in an ongoing process. You first become *AWARE* of the Word. That it is **God** speaking to you. Then, you get to KNOW the Word, so that:

   a) You can effectively *use* it when the need arises,
   b) So that the Holy Spirit can use it to teach and train you in the process of your spiritual growth. The Word itself is designed to lead you into a

deeper relationship with the Lord. It was given you so that you could learn to think God's thoughts after Him, cooperate with Him in fulfilling His Will for your life and those around you. It is also your *Weapon* against the enemy. The MOST powerful one we have. (Psa. 138:2) Then you must **APPLY** what you know. Like Nike says, *Just Do it*...

4) Finally, you must maintain a vital and fresh relationship with the Lord, through praise, worship, prayer, study and *confession of His Word daily.*

Now, let's get to work...

Table of Contents

Is There Not A Cause?..............................70

Paraclete...74

Boot Camp...75

Special Forces..82

Navy SEALS... 85

Perimeter Defense................................. 88

Tactics of the Enemy............................. 94

The First Step.. 96

Believer's Special Forces Creed...........100

What Do You Know About Satan's Tactics.........104

Staying Well Oiled and Ready.....................137

Is There Not a Cause?

The mugger pummeled the woman's husband till he couldn't move. Seeing her husband so brutalized, sent the woman into a frenzied panic.

The huge giant of a man wiped her husband's blood from his fist and slowly turned to face her.

"*Please!* " she begged. "Take the money and just *leave*! Leave us *alone! Please!*"

She had just gotten paid. She opened her purse and threw the handle full of 50's and 100's at him.

"Just *take it!*"

He bent over, picked up the smattering of bills, and calmly counted them right there on the darkened street as if he had all the time in the world..

"You've *got* everything that you wanted, now leave us alone," she said collapsing to the ground and covering her husband with a burst of tears.

He folded the money slowly, and then placed it in his pocket.

"I got what I wanted," he said in a deep and frightening tone, then added,

"..But that's not *all* that I wanted," he said walking towards her with a sadistic grin.

He grabbed the terrified woman by the throat and lifted her bodily from her crumpled position and said,

"Now, are you going to give me the *rest* of what I want... Or am I going to have to *take* it," he demanded, eyeing her up and down, much the way a horse trader examines a filly for his stable...

Behind him a quiet voice said with cold authority,

"Put the woman down—*now*. If you do, I will let you leave."

The Man Mountain turned slowly to see who would dare interrupt him as he queried,

"And if I *don't*?"

"Then, you will be *unable* to leave—*in one piece...*"

The huge mugger studied the man. He tossed the woman to the side like a sack of old clothes and pointed a stern finger at her like it was a gun.

"I'll get to you in a minute, don't you move. Stay right *there,* while I handle..*this."*

Turning his full attention to the small, diminutive man before him, he said,

"Let's see, no gun, no knife, no stick, no badge, or weapon of any kind. Hmph. I'd ask you your name, but I already know who you are—*dead meat!*" he screamed rushing at the little 5' 7" man.

The man moved like he was inside the mugger's head. He dodged every punch, anticipated every strike, and ducked every blow. His long hours of practice paid off as the 280-pound Goliath tried to kill him with every blow.

He blocked the last strike and struck with a swiftness that stunned mugger and observer alike. The powerful open palm strike caught the mugger square in the chest, in the middle of the sternum, quaking his heart.

The elusive bullet-quick stranger not only knew how to strike, but *where...*

The blow drove the air from the attackers lungs. The terrorizer suddenly knew terror. He collapsed to one knee, fighting to get his breath.

"Now," said the stranger calmly,

"Restore what you have stolen…"

The colossal man sputtered and cursed and swore and threatened, but all the while dug the woman's money from his pocket and left it on the ground.

"Now—*leave*."

The man struggled to his feet, then hurried off, realizing that on this particular night the old adage was true.

Crime *doesn't* pay...

The above scenario is carried out all over the country and around the world, day after day and night after night, in your city, in your town, in your country and in mine. Maybe even on your street and God forbid, maybe this or something similar to it, has even happened to you, a loved one or someone you know. But for *most* people, there was no stranger and master of *Kung Fu* to come along side to help...

Paraclete...

Statistics tell us that one out of so many citizens in our country, state or town will be assaulted. Optimists hope that they will be among the number that escapes being visited by such physical misfortune.

If you are a Christian however, you are assured of the fact that sooner or later you will be subject to a *spiritual* **assault** of some kind from the Enemy. And, regrettably, these kinds of assaults can be just as devastating as a physical one, if not more so.

These assaults can affect your family, your health, your marriage, your finances, your job, your business, your mind, your ministry, your dreams, your hopes, your visions, your emotions, your possessions, your very life and worst of all, your relationship with God. Consequently, these attacks, if one is unprepared for them, can leave one far more crippled and destroyed in life than some one who's physical wounds and scars have long since healed.

We have a *Spiritual Kung Fu* Instructor, if you will, who consistently pulls along side us to help us overcome in Life. He is the **Holy Spirit**. The Lord Jesus Christ said He has been sent, by the Father and the Son, to ***teach and train*** us in spiritual things, including how to take God's Manual For Life, **The Bible**, (His Kung Fu Manual if you will) and apply it *successfully* to our lives...

You may initially have a problem with the term 'Self' in Spiritual Self-Defense. Don't. You have to effectively learn how to apply the Word of God to your *own* life before you can ever effectively help anyone else! The Lord Jesus said: "Save your*self* from this untoward generation." Self is only a problem when you allow it to be by allowing it to come between you and the Lord and those He wants you to serve and minister to.

Boot Camp...

Welcome to God's Army

In the military, an individual is put through 8 weeks of Basic Training, then another 8 - 10 weeks in their particular MOS (area of specialty) where they receive advanced training in what will eventually become their particular job assignment.

First, however in Boot Camp the military teaches them the basics of what it takes to survive as an individual solider in the modern Army, Air Force, Navy or the Marines. Without a thorough knowledge of how to *survive* as an ***individual,*** he or she would never *live long enough* to function as a viable *part of a **Team...***

You as a Believer have to be aware of two things.

1) <u>**YOU**</u> are the one responsible for learning the Word and applying it to your life as an individual. Not your Pastor. Not your Bishop. Not your Rector. Not your Deacons. Not your Prophet, Evangelist or Teacher.
YOU are. These others are set as gifts in the Church to *help* you learn, but YOU are responsible for APPLYING what they *teach* you from the Word to your OWN life. They can*not* do it *for* you.

2) You are part of a TEAM. What you learn is not so that you use it exclusively for yourself. It's not all about you. It's about the

entire Body of Christ. The Body can only be as strong as its' weakest member. So, just like in the military, you learn *individual* survival skills so that you can protect yourself so that you can live and assist your unit and your squad, your platoon, your company, your battalion, etc, to *enforce* victory on the head of your enemy, Satan. Yes, he is defeated, but it's your job to *enforce* that defeat. Psa. 149:6-9. Who else is going to apply the power of God upside Satan's head? Who? The Buddhists? The Muslims? The Hare Krishnas? The Hindus? No. That leaves only one group left—*Christians*, you and me and the rest of the Body of Christ are the people God has chosen to do that.

3) You are *vital* as a Team Member in the Body of Christ. Your position in the Body of Christ is crucial. Your position in the Body of Christ is crucial all the way down to the very words that you *speak*. That's a key reason why the Lord said that we would stand judgement for every 'idle word that we speak'. Matt.12:36.

The Greek New Testament word translated idle, is 'argos'. It is translated in other places in the New Testament as: *Unprofitable, idle, slow, barren*. The Rotherham translation translates the above phrase: "..*every useless expression*" we will give account there of in Judgement." The greek word for judgement is "krisis". Sound familiar? It is the same word we get our word "crisis" from and means the same thing. What's the point? *The Lord is trying to tell us that every **negative** or **useless word** we use can lead us into, and force us into a position of "crisis" in our personal lives!*

Why? Because you have been given the power and authority to "command" and speak the awesome Word of God and change lives and circumstances, both as an individual and as a Team Member. And when we don't *fulfill our job and function*, it can affect the *whole* Team, Platoon, Company, and Battalion. Here's a simple example…

Pfc. Studdard stood guard at the vital Ikbein Bridge, a little known but critical link for the retreating German Army. General Vanhause had confided to his staff that morning that he knew the war was lost. That America and her allies were well on the way to winning the war, and since that was the case, they had nothing to lose. General Vanhause had received a desperate communiqué from the Furher that morning: *" Though the war may be lost, inflict as much damage as possible on advancing enemy troops. Make deception and destruction your staples and your life's bread. Take every opportunity and opening the advancing enemy gives you to devastate their ranks! Signed, Adolf Hitler."*

Vanhause hit upon a bold and daring plan…

Pfc. Studdard stood in front of the Ikbein Bridge and decided to relax and have a cigarette. The war was almost over, he reasoned, and there had been no activity in his area for weeks.

All was quiet.

He slung his rifle on his shoulder, lit up a butt and took a long drag on the cigarette. No one would know. He was out here all by himself. His Sgt. had given him strict orders to be on his guard.

No one must pass.

They were the rear guard element for the entire 7th Armour Division. They were the unit that secured the rear flank of the advancing tank element. It was vital this area stay secure while the tanks secretly refueled for a surprise attack they would launch against the retreating Germans within the next day or two.

"Studdard!" His Sgt. had said,

"*No one* gets pass you with out the password. Understood?"
"Sure Sarg!"
"Any one comes up to you, give the sign: He died for our sins. The counter sign is "Jesus Christ".
"Ok, yeah I got it."
"Good, you got a twelve hour shift."
"*Aw*, Sarg…"
"Save it Studdard. Count your blessings. You could be on the *Russian* front..."

That had been 10:00 this morning. It was now 9:00 PM. Another hour to go.

He heard a twig snap.
He dropped the glowing butt and stamped it out. The noise had taken him completely by surprise and frightened him.
He clumsily slung the rifle from his shoulder and pointed it into the total darkness in the direction of the sound.

"Halt! Who-who goes there, I mean--'He died for our sins…"

He heard the crunching of several pairs of boots headed in his direction.
"He died for our sins!" He shouted again.
The crunching got closer.
He raised the rifle nervously and sighted down the barrel, then doubt exploded in his mind like a bomb.
Suppose they're American! Suppose it's just some civilians or children lost in the dark! Suppose it's some soldiers who are so badly wounded, they can't talk!
The Sgt.'s words rang in his ears: "If they don't give the password, *they must not pass*!"
He sweated, pondering what to do while all the time the steps drew closer till they were nearly upon him.
One last time.

"He--"

"Hey buddy! Don't shoot! We're coming in!"

"You *American*??" Studdard queried.

"As apple pie!" A voice called back, "How 'bout those Yankees, huh? Wonder if they'll go anywhere this year, ya think?"

"I dunno, you know the Yankees," Studdard said lowering his weapon a little.

"Yeah, me and my boys got separated from our unit, been stumbling around in the dark for hours."

They sure *sounded* American...

Three dim figures emerged from the shadows directly in front of him and the bridge, all looking like dusty GI's.

They *looked* American...

The first one wore the stripes of a Lt.

Studdard hesitated...

The Lt. walked past him, the other two halted and stood waiting as Studdard turned to face the young blue-eyed Lt.

"Uhh, sir. I-I'm supposed to ask you for the counter sign..."

The Lt. turned and faced the confused Pfc.

"Of course you are," he said and nodded to one of the two men standing behind the trusting Pfc.

The knife stroke caught him completely by surprise and his rifle clattered to the ground as he pitched forward. Just before his life faded away, he saw the young Lt. smile at him and say,

"Heil Hitler, Private," with the slightest hint of a German accent, then he waved at someone across the way in the bushes and said,

"The coast is clear General Vanhause, come ahead! The guard was *no problem at all*!"

Vanhause grinned broadly at the success of his plan and waved his second in command on, and the entire 3rd Panzer Division rumbled across the Ikbein Bridge and attacked the 7th US

Armored Div. from the rear at the most vulnerable time, while in the midst of refueling. The 3rd Panzer rolled up the entire rear flank of the 7th Div like a window shade. The losses were staggering, and it took an entire month to halt the thundering advance of a rejuvenated Gen. Vanhause...

All because one person didn't *apply* what he knew...
He did not see the big picture. He never realized how *vital* he really was.

You are *not* in the place, job, house, church or neighborhood or family you are in, just because you *happened* to be there. You hold a vital position in the Body of Christ. Your prayers could be guarding the rear of the Body of Christ from attack. You MUST keep your guard up and be on the ready. You are not there even to reach just one soul. As incredibly important as that is, there's something even *more* important. **SOULS**--plural! It's time we stopped thinking small. I'm here to affect one person? No, you're here to affect hundreds and thousands for the Kingdom. If you think you'll never amount to much, *you won't*. If you realize that your single prayer can affect *thousands, it will...*

Your prayers can prevent a Pastor from falling into sin, an Evangelist from dying in a plane crash, a Missionary from a crippling car accident, and a Pastor's wife from cancer, a Christian brother or sister from a mugging or even worse, murder.

It can prevent a family from being destroyed, a church from bankruptcy, a Ministry from financial ruin, a child from being born crippled. Are you *solely* responsible for the success or failure of *every single person* in the entire world?

No.

But are you the one on **Guard Duty** for *your* family, *your* job, *your* Pastor and *your* Church, your Bishop, your country and the Body?

Yes.

You are part of a *Team* as a member of your church, or any church. IF every Team member feels their part is *insignificant*, they will not do their job or fulfill their responsibilities.

But, do you know what?

If you don't have any *confidence* in your prayers for your*self* or your own family, you won't have *any confidence* in your prayers for any one *else* and a gap appears it the defenses of the Body of Christ…

But my prayers won't amount to anything…
If you *think* that way, they won't, but Satan *knows* better…
And so should you…

The stronger you are as an ***individual*** in the Power of the Lord, the *stronger* will be your family, your prayer life and your Church. Because each *Team* can only be as strong as it's *members*.

Your Squad is your family.
Your Platoon is your extended family.
Your Company is your Bible Study or Prayer Group
Your Battalion is your Church.
Your Division is the AO (Area of Operations in the Body of Christ you are assigned.)
Your Battalion Commanders are your Pastors
PRAY for them all.
Your C&C (Commander and Chief): Is the Lord Jesus Christ…

Remember that.

Special Forces...

In nearly every military in the world, there are conventional forces and *Special* Forces.
The same is true for the Body of Christ.

Let's look at the difference between Conventional forces and Special Forces, and how that applies to us...

Strategy and Tactics...

Conventional military forces and Special Forces respond differently to the exact same kind of situations.

Ambush...

In Vietnam there was a very deadly and devastating ambush known as the "L-Shaped Ambush". It was named thus, because it was shaped like an 'L' lying on it's side.

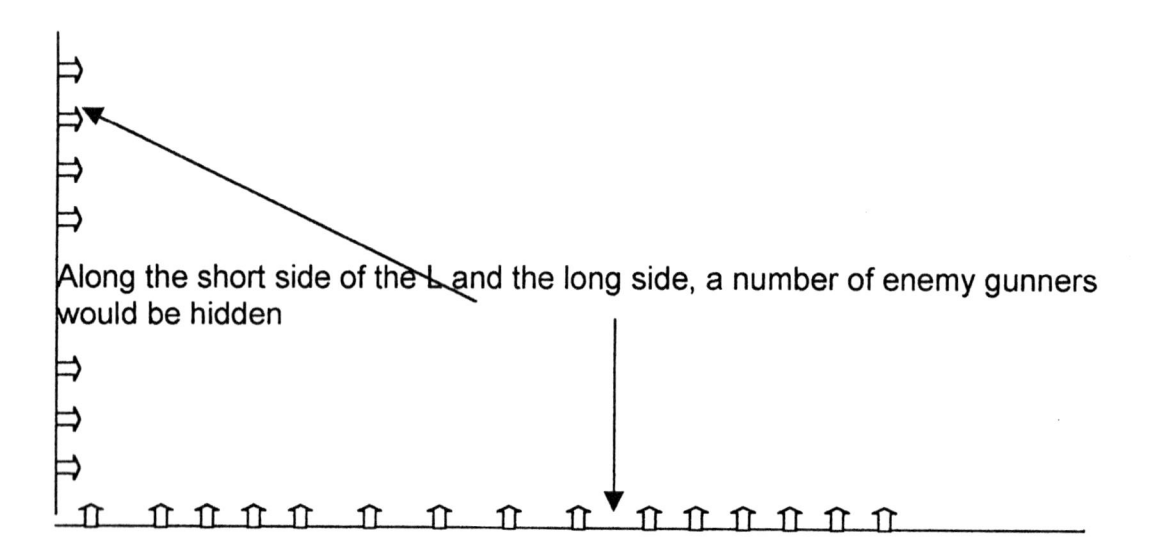

Along the short side of the L and the long side, a number of enemy gunners would be hidden

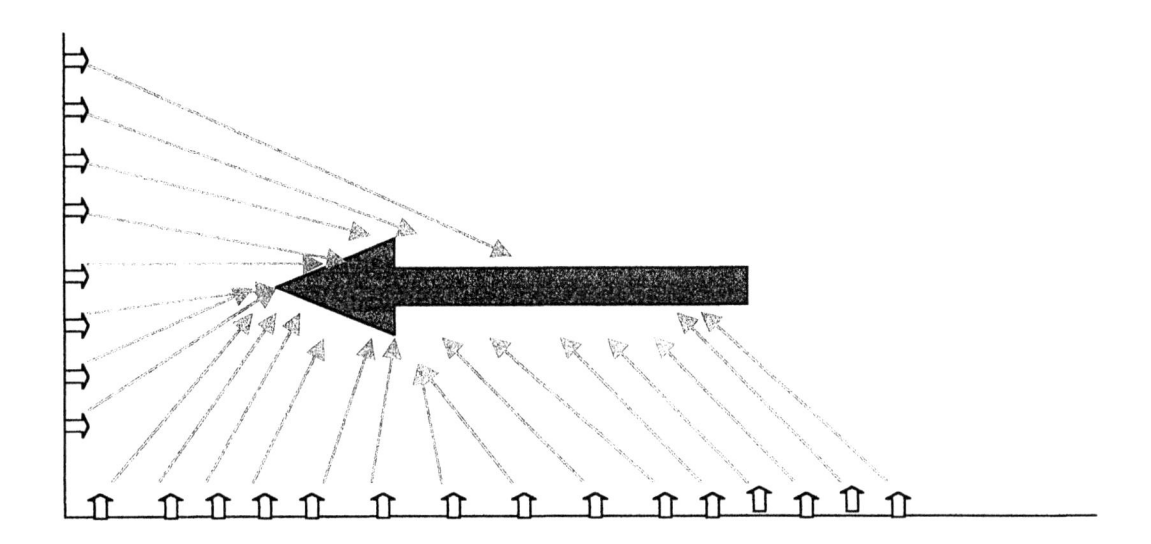

An American patrol would be baited to enter into the 'L', where enemy soldiers would be camouflaged and out of sight.

They would have a 'rabbit' sometimes as bait—a scared looking Viet Cong, who would run away to *draw* the soldiers into the trap. Once our troops were deep into the trap, or "kill zone" as it was also known, the enemy would open fire on all sides.

Usually a patrol that found itself in an ambush endeavored to withdraw and regroup so that it could call in air strikes and/or artillery...

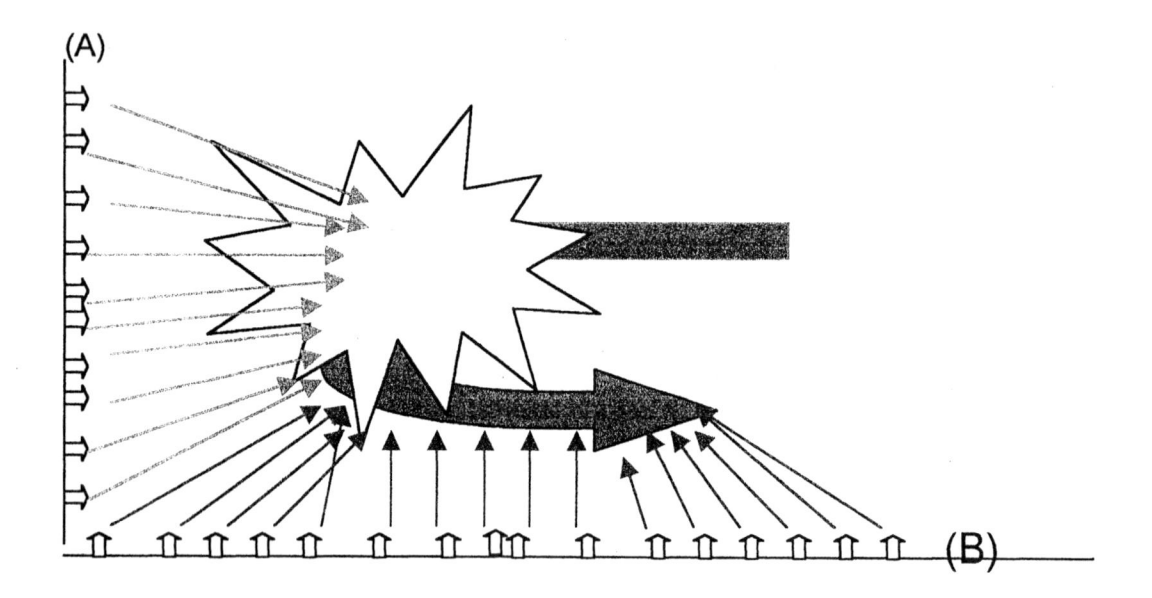

The Viet Cong and NVA, knowing this, would fire along the *short* side (A) of the "L" *first*. Then, as the patrol would move to their left running for cover or attempt to withdraw, the <u>rest</u> of the ambush--along the long side (B) of the "L", would open up with <u>*everything*</u> they had with withering fire and devastating effect...

And many times the <u>*whole platoon*</u> would be destroyed...

Navy Seal Team Tactics…

Faced with the same situation, Navy Seals never fell for the "rabbit trick". If they did however *inadvertently* walk into an ambush, they applied a totally different combat doctrine and strategy…

As soon as they realized they had walked into an ambush, they **attacked** the ambush and "charged" straight ahead!

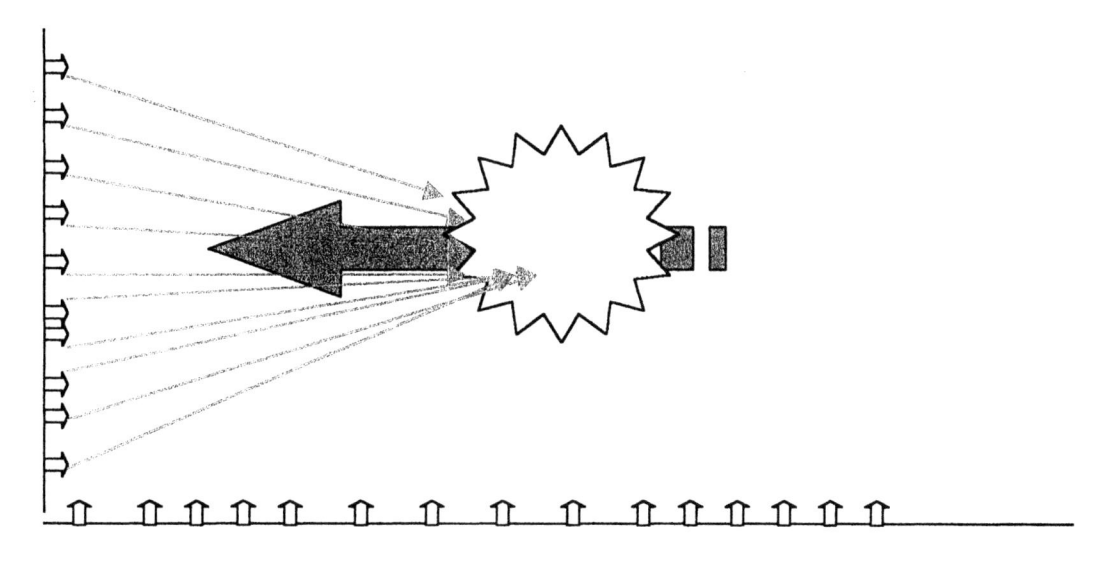

The SEAL team surges **forward** firing all weapons and throwing grenades. They catch an over *confident* enemy *completely* by surprise. The enemy expected them to become confused, alarmed, and to attempt to *withdraw*, and thus fall into the *rest* of their trap. The enemy expected them to simply die.

Instead, they **attacked**, in force, and fought *through* the enemy…

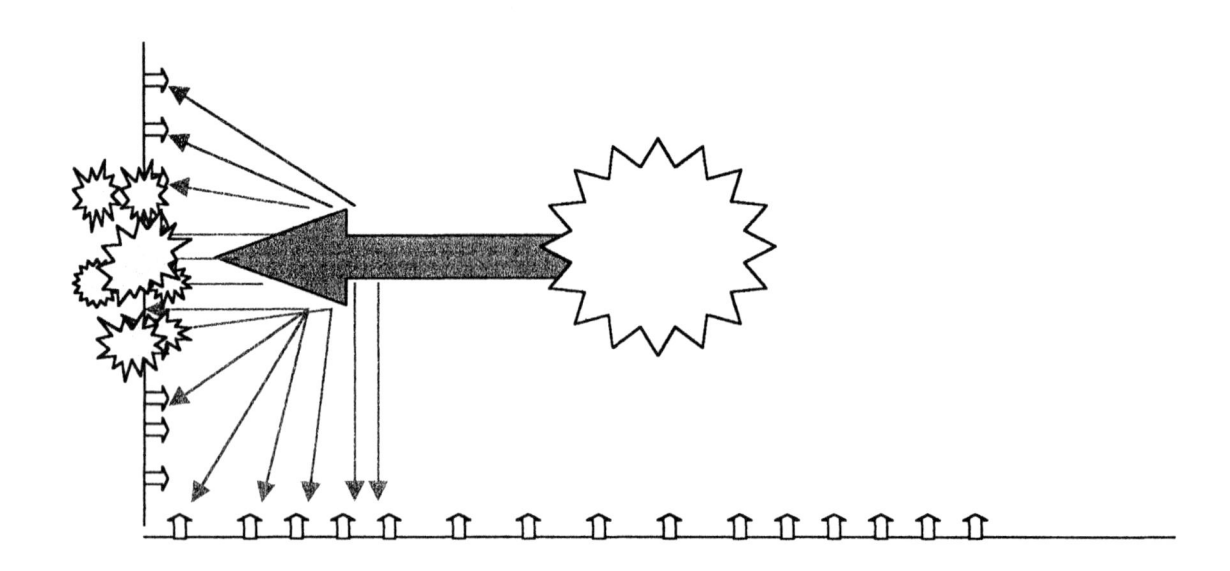

The SEAL Team surges *toward* the enemy fire unleashing accurate and massively *intense firepower*. Enemy troops directly in front of them either break and run, or are **terminated!**

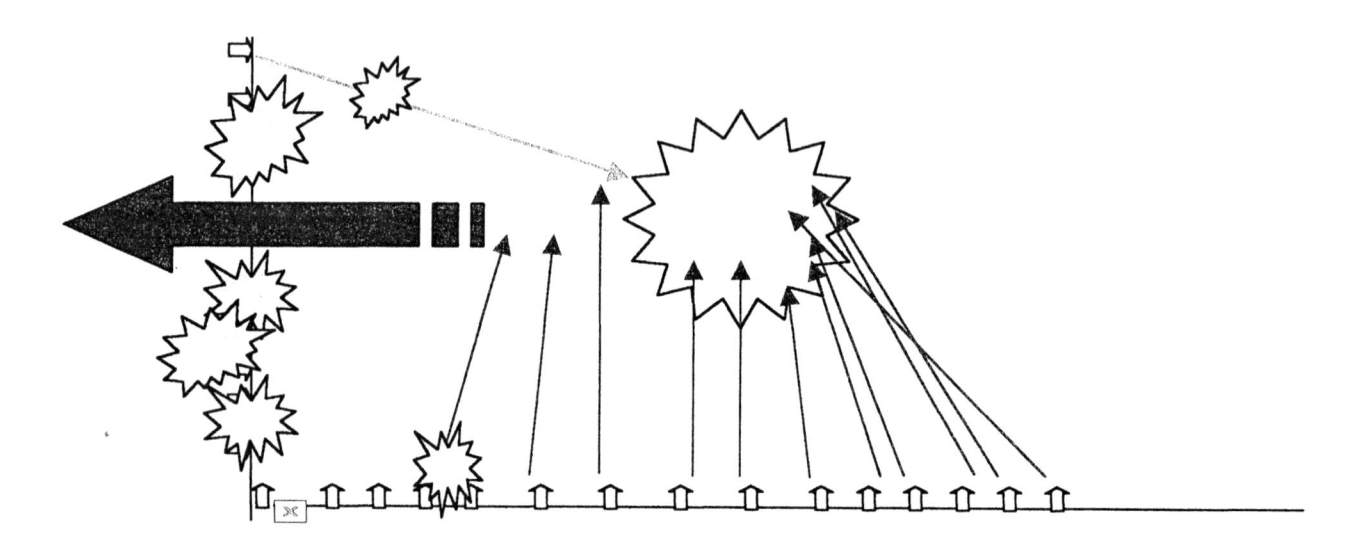

Sometimes they moved so swiftly that they were already through and *out of* the ambush before the rest of the enemy even knew! It left the Enemy firing in the wrong place!

Seal Teams did the *opposite* of what the enemy expected. The enemy was use to troops that withdrew and hunkered down, not troops that *immediately* **attacked!**

The very same thing is true regarding Satan, our enemy. He is so use to the Body of Christ 'retreating to regroup' that he lies in wait with traps for those who withdraw under his 'fire'—fiery darts! But he is totally *unprepared* for an anointed, ***aggressive*** **attack** of committed, focused men and women of God...

Always remember this: Hesitation in *ANY* self-defense situation, spiritual, or physical, *ALWAYS* gives an enemy, both opportunity and *incentive* to attack you!

Don't hesitate.

When Satan attacks *you* or your family or loved ones with, sin, sickness, disease, depression, anxiety, financial woes, temptations, tests and trials, *attack him back*—***immediately!***

Remember that, and practice it...

Perimeter Defense

Your home is your 'Base of Operations'. How well defended is your "Base Camp'?

In Vietnam, the US Military had what they called "FOB's"—Forward Operations Bases. They were also called FB's or "Fire Bases" for short. The soldiers within them fortified these bases against enemy attack. The bases where the commanders dug in deep, stayed alert, and kept their troops alert, and maintained an upgrading of their defenses—survived. Those that did *not*, for whatever reason, did *not* survive.

YOU are in a *real* war too, how well prepared are your defenses, spiritually, mentally, emotionally, financially, physically, professionally against an attack from Satan and his minions? How well prepared are *you* against his onslaught of sickness, disease, financial ruin, marital problems, emotional stress, etc?

As a man or woman of God, just like in the military, *YOU* are the one responsible for preparing your family against Satan's attacks. How good a job are you doing? They are depending on *you*. God's Power and His Word and His Spirit are available to you and *for* you to help defend you. But do you know that He expects **YOU** to **apply** these factors to your life? **HE** does *His* part, but we must come to realize that He also expects us to do **OURS**!

Let's look at what tools Our Heavenly Father and the Lord Jesus Christ have provided for us, and how to use them…

Actively *Apply* the Blood of Jesus To Your Life

Job 22:28 says, "*Thou* shalt decree a thing and it shall be established unto thee." **Decree**, loudly and with authority that the Blood of the Lord Jesus Christ provides an impenetrable defense around you. That Satan and his minions have to "pass-over" you, because of the Blood. Ex. 12:21-23.

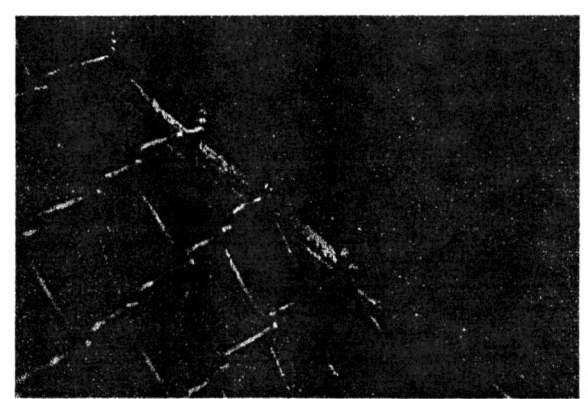

Surround your home and family with the 'Barbed Wire' of the **Word of God** by *Applying* that Word through the ***Blood* of Jesus**.
You will find on page 100 a sample of a Confession of God's Word. You can also establish and write down your own—personalize it!

Remember, Satan is a *thief* and a *murderer*. A true spiritual *psycho* who will not pass up *any* open door you give him to come in and steal and kill and destroy you or your family. The Word says in Eph. 4:27: *Neither give place* (we could safely say an 'open door') *to the devil…*

Stop leaving the door open and the 'spiritual welcome mat' out, Because he will surely come in.

He's like a carnivorous spiritual animal *looking* for any way into your life or home that you will give him. Don't sin! If you are involved in any sin, *stop it* **immediately** and kill it **NOW**. It is not only an open door; it is a huge *hole* in the Hedge of God's protection around you!

It is your job as a man or woman of God to keep Satan at bay by using all the weapons and fire power that God has placed at your disposal. As a Believer you are responsible for applying the Weapons that the Father has given you for just such an occasion and purpose as this…

The Warrior's Agenda Combat Study Guide—Part 2, by David M. Humphrey Sr,
thewarriorsagenda.com, ©Copyright 2003

Satan and his minions consider themselves ready for conflict…

But how ready and prepared ARE you?

Make up your mind, that being a soldier in God's army is good...

But being a **Warrior** in the Army of God is **Better**... Why?

Because a soldier in the Army of God will usually do whatever he *can*. But a **Warrior** in the Army of God, will do

...What ever it **TAKES**...

Tactics of the Enemy
No.1: Distractions

One of the most dangerous things that we as Christians have to be aware of is the enemy's ability to distract us. We have to realize that we are actually engaged in a daily spiritual contest of epic proportions against intelligent beings that desire our complete destruction.

How the Tactic of Distraction Works

Satan and his minions know for a fact that no Born Again Christian with 2 ounces of sense would turn around and serve Satan voluntarily. Every Christian that the Lord has commissioned to fulfill a task for Him hits the ground running, but then along the way they slow down, get discouraged, get off track, get distracted and then sometimes awake to find themselves far off the course that they had started on for the Lord and wondering how they got there. Others of us have found ourselves mired back in some of the woes and sin that we had escaped from. How did that happen? No Born Again Christian is trying to find a way off course and into sin or defeat. Born Again Christians are seeking a way out! So how do some Christians, sometimes mature believers, end up off course? We know that it was with the help of the devil, but for the most part we as believers never stopped to listen to our Father or the Lord long enough to find out *how*. We have a saying at our ministry that the Lord gave me at its very inception: **Only Forward—*Never* Back!**

I have endeavored to maintain that forward momentum and attitude at every turn, but I found myself at one point, discouraged, off course, ineffective and playing catch up to the things and the schedule that the Lord had given me to fulfill. The Holy Spirit sat me down and opened up to me this very simple but effective tactic of the enemy and that very day I sat down and at His behest put it in this book.

The Tactic of Distraction

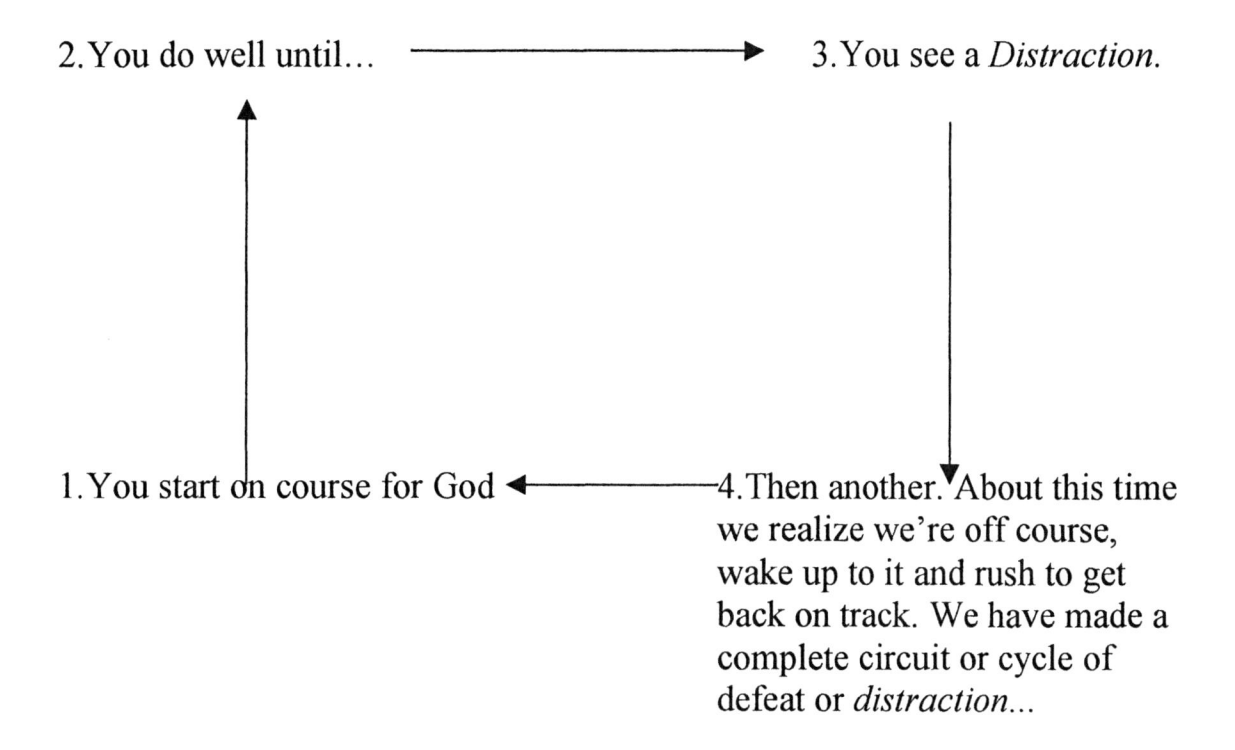

2. You do well until... ⟶ 3. You see a *Distraction*.

1. You start on course for God ⟵ 4. Then another. About this time we realize we're off course, wake up to it and rush to get back on track. We have made a complete circuit or cycle of defeat or *distraction*...

The First Step

Let's take a closer look at this deceptive process. You start off gung ho about what the Lord has called you to do. It may be ministry, a business, starting a Bible study, an invention, a book, a newsletter, tape ministry or whatever the Lord has told you to do.

You start off fired up. **But,** somewhere along the way you find that it's not quite as *easy* as you thought it would be...

If it's a business or ministry, you find there's a surprising amount of paperwork and activity that has to be done first.
No matter what the dream is that the Lord placed on your heart or told you to do, you will find that there is an amazing amount of work involved.

When you are involved in doing the things of God, one of the consistencies you will find—no matter what your dream or commission from God— is that you will have to deal with...

people.

People as a whole can be your greatest *blessing* and at the same time can be your greatest *challenge*.

You will find that...

Some people will be pulling *for* you, and some will be pulling *against* you. Either way, you have to remember that ultimately what God has given you to do, will be a blessing to people, but, you can not afford to direct your ministry or your business or your God given vision by what people *think* of you, or of your vision. Because, if you do, then at that point, *people* are ones directing your God-given vision, not God and not you.

You cannot afford to let that happen. You are to be led by the *Spirit of God, not* the opinions or facial expressions of people. You also cannot afford to allow your vision to be directed by the varying levels of commitment of people OR the *lack* there of.

Sometimes the people who are supposed to be committed to you, may lack true commitment. Don't get discouraged. You may feel like forgetting them and moving on. *I'll just do everything myself!* But you will find that when God calls you to do something that will bless people, if it's big enough, you're going to need people to help you with getting it done!

PRAY FOR YOUR PEOPLE! PRAY FOR THEIR FAMILIES AND YOURS! Satan attacks *them*, just like he does *you*. In fact the strategy is, take out the people one by one, and then he hopes you will get discouraged, (and guess what, discouragement is a *distraction!*). He hopes you will then turn in the direction of that distraction and concentrate on the distraction *more* than on your mission and your vision!

Step Two

A distraction doesn't have to be sin all the time to be effective in getting you off track from your vision...

Infact, sometimes the most effective distraction from Satan's standpoint isn't a sin at all!

Discouragement is a distraction that can stop you dead in your tracks. If you allow it to continue it can lead to depression, confusion, despair and the like. Your people see you discouraged or confused and they respond in the same manner, because in whatever direction the head *leans*, that's the way the body will go! They will follow your example, consciously or not.

I use to be a professional driving instructor at one time and one of the most interesting things that I have ever discovered is that when you're driving, as a beginner or even as an experienced driver, is this fact: In whatever direction you are *looking*, that is the direction your car will eventually start heading in. If you look out the window to the left for an extended period of time, 20 seconds or more, your car will start slowly easing to the left. Not a full turn, just a slight easing to the left and over the line. Same thing is true if you look right, your car will drift that way into some else's lane!

Where ever you concentrate your *attention*, that's where your life and ministry will begin to go and if you don't look straight ahead again, you're headed for a crash... Keep your eyes on the Lord and His Word!

Your Special Forces Creed...
(Based on the creed of the US Army Rangers and the US Special Forces)

Special Forces means I recognize the fact that I have volunteered and have been chosen as one of the elite of the Kingdom of God. Being Born Again and chosen as a Special Forces operative I will always endeavor to uphold the prestige, honor and high "Espirit De Corps" of my *Regiment* which is my church_____. Gallantly will I show the world that I'm a specially selected and well-trained Warrior in the Army of God. My courtesy to superior officers; my Pastor, Bishop, Teacher, etc., neatness of dress and care of equipment shall set the example for others to follow. Above all I will reach my objective honorably, I WILL NEVER CHEAT to obtain a victory but instead always obey The Word of God.

Pride in my Savior, my Heavenly Father, His Word, my Church, the Body of Christ, my Family, my Team and Myself will always lead my actions. Never shall I fail my comrade's. I will always keep myself mentally alert, physically strong and morally straight and I will shoulder more than my share of the task whatever it may be. One Hundred-percent and then some. I will be their eyes and ears, working as one TEAM, one entity.

Ever vigilant of the dangers to the Body of Christ, the Church, my leaders, my family, my team should they be flanked, I will provide back-up to any & all of the above and my team members, and constantly watch their backs when they are engaged in fire, i.e. under attack from the enemy. I will pray for them daily "before" sickness, *disease or tragedy happens. I will listen to the Holy Spirit. I will be the eyes in the back of their head as they will be the eyes in the back of mine.*

C *ourageously and Energetically will I meet the enemies of the Kingdom of God, the Body of Christ, my Family and my Country. Acting without mercy I shall defeat the works of Satan on the field of battle, for the Lord Jesus Christ has already defeated him and I am Spirit Filled and sent to ENFORCE that defeat with the Power of the Holy Spirit. And because I have the Holy Spirit within me, I am better trained by Him than my enemy is, and I will fight with all my might and according to the Word of God. Because it is written: FIGHT THE GOOD FIGHT OF FAITH and BE STRONG IN THE LORD AND THE POWER OF HIS MIGHT! His might, is now MY Might, because He has given it to me. I will always maintain that I am a member of the Body of Christ, my Church, my Family, my Study Group and my Team and never just an individual.*

I *will train endlessly… in the Word of God, mastering each weapon of my warfare available to me by the Holy Spirit and the Word of God, for these are the tools of my trade. I will choose my weapons (my words and my prayers) carefully as to compliment my team and enhance the effectiveness of it to complete our objective.*

A *cknowledging the fact that as a Special Forces Elite Warrior I will arrive at the cutting edge of battle by Prayer, The Word of God and the Principles there of, including the Word of Command, (Job 22:28, Rom 4:17, Joshua 10:12 and Mark 11:23) moving further, faster and fight harder than any other soldier. I accept that my Savior, the Lord Jesus Christ, my Heavenly Father, my Pastor, my Church, my Family, my Country and my Team members expect me to be in place and do my part to complete the mission successfully. I will never leave my team in jeopardy while maintaining my own safety over the safety of the team.*

L *oyalty to my chain of command (Father, Son, and Holy Spirit), superiors; Pastor, Teachers, etc., and allegiance to the force of the Word of God and His Power, is engrained in my soul! I will **never***

overstep my authority. My superiors lead and I will follow! I will never question their authority aslong as they maintain a life of Holiness before God and believe in and adhere to the inerrant Word of God and will never degrade them when speaking to others. I recognize the fact that I am accountable 24 hours a day to the Lord Jesus Christ for my words and my actions as a Christian and Special Forces Team Member in the Body of Christ. Therefore I will always carry my self as an honorable man or woman of God and obey His Word and leading.

One Lord, One Faith, One Baptism!

We are **One force, One team, One person… Unbeatable**. We are members of the **Body of Christ**. I will perform the impossible. Be where others cannot be, see where others cannot see, act when others are afraid to act. My team is my lifeblood and I am theirs. If I fail, my team, my church, my pastor, my leaders, my family, my loved ones are jeopardized… Therefore I will NOT fail!

*Precision accuracy is foremost… My bullets are my words. I have the Power of Life and Death in my Tongue! Prov 18:21. I will place each shot on target whether it be as a sniper or lead infantry (i.e., whether I pray by myself or in a group). I will choose every word carefully identifying each target as the Enemy **before** releasing my lethal verbal payload. I will not be guilty of using my words to destroy other members of the Body of Christ. I will never fire my words recklessly as to jeopardize any of my team to "Friendly Fire". I will always walk in Love, in word and deed.*

Surrender is not a Special Forces word. I will Never fail to respond to the call of a comrade needing my assistance and prayer, encouragement or support, knowing they will always respond to mine. I will never leave a fallen comrade to fall into the hands of sin and the Enemy and under no circumstances will I ever embarrass my Lord and Savior Jesus Christ, my Heavenly Father, the Holy Spirit, my Church, my Pastor, my Leaders, my Family, my Country, the prestigious name of the Body of Christ, or my Team….

Signed_____Dated_____

The War College ©2003
The Warrior's Agenda©2003

I am a Special Forces Spiritual Warrior. I am a Warrior of the Word. I am a Son or Daughter of the Living God, and I serve the Lord Jesus Christ…

Only Forward—*Never* Back…

The Warrior's Agenda Combat Study Guide Cont.

A New Dimension in Spiritual Warfare...

Satan's Tactics:

What Do You Know About Satan's *Tactics*?

The Apostle Paul wrote to the early church, "…Lest Satan should get an advantage of us: for we are not ignorant of his devices." 2 Corth. 2:11.

Paul admonished the early church to not be *ignorant* of Satan's devices. How much more should that be true of the Church as a whole *today*!

Sadly however, most of the church today *is* ignorant of his devices. Not because the Holy Spirit isn't ready to teach us and make us aware. Not because the Word doesn't have everything we need to know about Satan's devices and what to do about them. But sadly it's because we don't study. There are those that don't know…

And there are those that don't *want* to know…

But Brother Humphrey, I'm saved and spirit-filled, I don't need to know anything about how Satan works to kill and steal and to destroy. I don't need to know that.

In warfare, that kind of attitude will get you killed.

Imagine a Green Beret or Navy Seal or Recon Marine during the Viet Nam War saying,

"Aww, I don't need to know anything about the Viet Cong! I don't need to know anything about my enemy, his tactics, methods, his weapons or how he thinks."

Any soldier that thinks that way during wartime ends up very dead, very fast, killed as much by their *ignorance* as the enemy bullet that they were actually *shot* with.

Yeah, well, maybe you're right about that Brother Humphrey, but THAT's in real warfare."

And just what do you think *this* is?

That's why the Lord said in Hosea 4:6, **"MY PEOPLE, are <u>DESTROYED</u> for *LACK OF KNOWLEDGE.*"**

Notice. The Lord didn't say '*somebody else's*" people were destroyed for lack of knowledge, but He said *HIS* people were being destroyed by a lack of knowledge. And who's the Destroyer?

Well, I'm sorry. I just don't believe that. I don't accept that. I don't want to hear anything about Satan's devices.

Fine. That's ok. That's why the Lord wrote the *second* part of Hosea 4:6 for every one that might feel that way.

Second part?? What second part?

You see, while most of us quote that verse, we forget, that that's only the *first* part. The second part says:

"…Because thou hast "<u>rejected</u>" knowledge, I will also <u>reject thee</u>, that thou shalt be no priest to me: seeing thou hast forgotten the Law (the Word) of thy God, I will also forget thy children…"

Ouch. Strong ain't it.

Do you see now how *serious* our Father is about **you** *not* being ignorant of the Word *and* not being ignorant of Satan's devices?

I'm *not* talking about going out and studying sin or witchcraft or some such. No. Everything that we really *need* to know about his devices is already in the Word, but you *have to* study it, and *apply* it!

Well, yeah I know Brother Humphrey, but...

Ah, yes, the inevitable "*but*". I told a believer one time who kept "but-ing" everything that the Word was saying that, **"*Satan has the biggest "butt" in the world. And if you let him, he'll stick it right in your mouth.*"**

What does that mean? That if you find yourself "but-ing" what the Word tells you to do, like it or not, you're playing right into the devil's hands and everytime he offers you a 'but' to what the Word says, you're allowing Satan to take his 'but' and fit it into your lips.

Satan is a "technocrat". He loves confusing, abusing and misusing Christians (and killing them if he can) on "technicalities". He studies you, to see if you really *know* the Word, or just *think* you do.

Let's do a little test, and I'll show you what I mean.

With*OUT* turning in your Bible, let's see just how much Word you have correctly in your ***heart.***

Finish the following verses…

1) _____ is the root of all evil. 1 Tim 6:10.

2) My people _____ for lack of knowledge. (That's right, we just went over it, but I want to see how well you remember it.) Hosea 4:6

3) The anointing _____ the yoke. Isa. 10:27

4) Is not this the _____ that I have chosen…and that _____ yoke? Isa. 58:6

5) No weapon that is formed against thee shall prosper; and every tongue that shall rise against thee in judgement _____ shall condemn. This is the heritage of the servants of the Lord, and their righteousness is of Me, saith the Lord. Isa. 54:17

6) They that observe (give heed to) lying vanities _____ their own mercy. Jonah 2:8.

7) The Lord said "If you take one step, I'll take two." Where is this found in the Bible?

All verses are from the King James Version…

1) Money is *not* the root of all evil. The *love of* of money is.

2) We just covered this one at the start of this lesson. If you forgot this one already, you need to just go ahead and spank *yourself!* Because at that rate, the devil would consider you a "Happy Meal"!

3) The Word does *NOT* say the Anointing *breaks* the yoke. It says the Anointing **<u>Destroys</u>** the yoke.

4) *Is not this the "Fast" that I have chosen. That ye "Break" every yoke. So Fasting "breaks" the yoke. But the Anointing <u>Destroys</u> it.*

5) *THOU!* <u>YOU</u> shall condem it. There are a myriad of things that the Lord does *for* us, but as a Mature, Born Again, **Spirit-Filled** Believer, there are some things now that He expects *us* to do for *ourselves*.

6) "Forsake"

7) *If you find this one let me know, because in over 44 years of reading the Bible, beginning when I was 7 years old, I've never seen it or come across it anywhere.*

Satan's Tactics:

Spyware...

In the computer world, there's been a lot of talk about "spyware". Basically spyware is a mini program that attaches itself to your computer from over the internet with out your consent or knowledge. Spyware can do eveything from simply track where you *go* while you're on the internet, to actually *steal* your passwords and address book and secretly pass them over the internet while you're online, back to the person who *sent* you the program.

Satan has his own "spyware".

Demonic spirits that watch your "habits". How you think, how you react, what you do, where you go, how you pray (or *not*), how you study (or *not*).

Religious Spirits watch how you respond to the Word when it's taught or preached. Do you receive it? Believe it? Reject it? Or accept it.

Always remember, *Satan* is the Tempter, Tester, and Tryer—not God. James 1:13.

Religious Spirits study you and watch you to see if you will believe the lie: ***"This is God doing this to you, testing you, making you sick, making life hard, holding up your money…"***

Because they know that if you believe the lie, then…

They can do what ever they *want* to you by way of tempation, test and trial and you won't resist, you won't fight back with the *Word*,

Because you'll think it's "*God*" doing it to you and not *them*, which is *exactly what they* **want** *you to think!* 2 Kings 18:25, James 1:13

Spirits of Anger and Wrath, watch how you react to people they send to you and across your path to make you angry and upset.

Will you curse? Will you seek revenge? Will you gossip to other believers? Will you speak the Word? Will you *do* the Word? They seek to know and find out, what you will do. Will you take it out on a family member? Will you try to *break* something?

What will you do?

Spirits of Lust watch and wait. Will you watch what you're not supposed to on TV tonight? Will you yield to the advances of some one they send along who is not your husband or your wife. Some one that makes it clear they are interested in only *one* thing, and it's *not* to get to know you better. In addition, Porn on the internet is at epidemic levels in the world today. Will you fall for it...They say: *Just once...Awww, no one will ever know...We won't tell...*

Pornography, for those who listen to the lies of this Spirit, becomes terribly addictive, and many a marriage has fallen prey to Satan's minions because of someone who was only going to look "one time"...

Our society is plagued by time spent traveling too fast, too many things to do and not enough time. Consequently when some people finally *do* slow down, they find themselves lonely, depressed and feeling empty. So, as a substitute, many turn to "food" for company, to fill the emptiness. It is then that a ***Spirit of Glutonny*** using loneliness as a tool, tries to get a person, Christian or non-Christian, to make their stomach thier"god"…

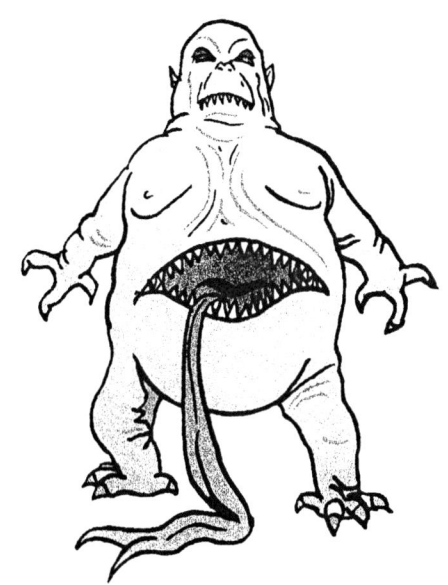

Paul said: "All things are lawful unto me, but all things are not expedient. All things are lawful unto me, but I will NOT be brought under the power of any."

In other words, Paul said, 'I rule my body and it's appetites. It does *not* rule me.'

You must remember, that you are a called and *Anointed Warrior of the Kingdom of God,* and that God our Father created *YOU* to **Rule** Principalities and Powers, Thrones and Dominions and over all the power, devices, tricks, *"spyware"*, and weapons of the enemy—so **Rule!!!** *Now*, not just in the *future*, but right **NOW**, in your Life, your Body, your Health, your Finances, your Home. The Lord Jesus Christ made you a ruling King and Priest—*be one. Nothing* should rule you but the Lord Jesus Christ, the Father God and His Spirit. Luke 10:19, Rev. 5:10, Rev. 1:5&6.

We walk in love toward our family, or loved ones, other Believers and the world. *BUT* we **Rule the Devil** and his crew, Luke 10:19, **Jer. 51:20**, we do not walk in love or passivity with evil spirits, but in *Power* and an *Attitude—an <u>Attitude of Dominion</u>…*

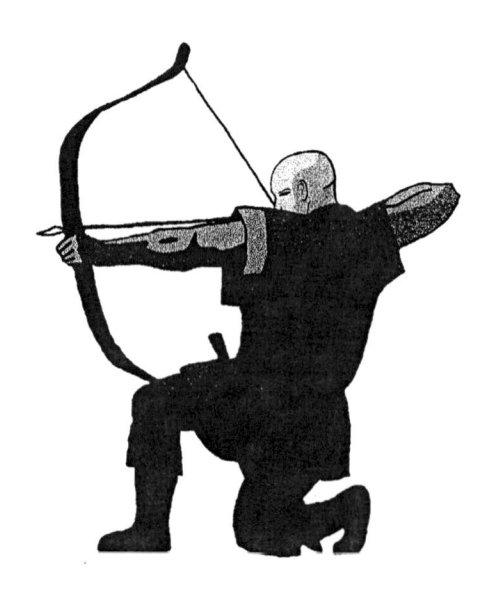

Satan's Tactics:

The Psychology of the Enemy

How Your Enemy Thinks...

Little, if any, thought has been given by most Believers to the *psychology*, of the Enemy. How he thinks, how he operates, his purposes, etc.

How about you? Have you ever stopped to think about *how* your Enemy operates? The reasons *behind* what he does? Or do you just rush off to respond to his attacks 'helter-skelter', with out ryhme or reason, *nor* listen to the Holy Spirit's advice on what to do? Most people respond to every attack of Satan, the same way; without insight or understanding. Have you ever taken the time to sit down and listen to the Holy Spirit and let Him *show* you the manner and the "pattern" Satan and his minions attack in?

In the military, once you notice the 'pattern' of an enemy. It makes it easier to defend against him the next time he comes *and* it makes it easier to *ambush* him…

We should be atleast that smart.

Let's look at some things that the Word says about him and his minions that can help us to turn the tide of battle in our lives…

Satan's Tactics:

Why Some Attacks Come...

Intelligence Gathering

Some attacks come because Satan and his minions want to find out how you will *respond*. They are seeking information. They want to find out how you will *behave* when you are attacked. *Will you run? Will you hide? Will you cry? Will you run to the Lord, or, will you* **attack, will you fight?** This information is *vital* to Satan and his demons.

We have to realize that we have been *lied to* by Satan and his crew. The average Christian today who does not know his or her Bible thinks that Satan and his demons can 'read our minds'. *Not* if you're saved and born again. 1 Cor. 2:11-12 & 16. Verse 16 says we *have* the "Mind of Christ". So, if Satan can read the Mind of Christ, then he can read your mind. But since he can't read *His*, that means he can *not* read yours..

Well, if that's the case Bro. Humphrey how does he know—

You *tell him...*

What do you mean 'I' tell him?

Satan and his minions *don't know* everything. They only know what they have gleaned from observing and interacting with human nature over the centuries—*and* what you and I have *blabbed* to them.

Let's look at Proverbs 28:16a.

"The Prince that <u>wanteth understanding</u> is also a <u>great oppressor</u>..."

We know from Ephesians 6:12 that there are various ranks of evil spirits. Principalities, Powers, Rulers of the Darkness of this World and Spiritual Wickedness in High (Grk: Heavenly) Places.

Principalities are *not* the first level of evil spirits, they are the first level of Evil Spirits that have major"*rank*". They are like "*Captains*". **Powers** are like "*Majors*", **Rulers** are like "*Colonels*" and **Spiritual**

Wickedness in High Places are like *"Generals"* and of course, Satan is their Commander.

There are millions of evil spirits, those with rank, and those with *no rank*, minor spirits, that endeavor to *harrass and distract* us. But principly, the broad majority of "buck privates" (harrassing spirits) are sent to control and keep the world's inhabitants in Darkness. Those with *serious rank* are sent against *us*. Satan considers the lost no problem. It's *us* he's worried about. So, as Paul points out, we are confronting his "officers" (Principalities, Powers, Rulers of the Darkness, etc.) who try to 'organize' and then lead 'ground' troops against us.

But, in any war, you need to know what your enemy is thinking and planning. You need to know his strengeths and you should know his weaknesses. So, in the military you launch "probing attacks" to find out; his troop strength, morale, tactics, experience, response time, etc.

Prov. 28:16 reveals to us that *when a Prince or Principality 'lacks understanding' about us; where we are in Christ, our level of spiritual maturity, our level of understanding of the Word, our "spiritual morale" our attitude, our strengths, our weaknesses, our manner of response to attacks, our spiritual guts and courage, then he brings an attack, "oppression" against us to judge our reactions and to find these things out!*

"The Prince that wanteth (or lacks) understanding (about you and where you are in Christ, in terms of maturity and strength) is also

a "great oppressor" (brings oppression—an attack, physically, mentally, finacially, maritally, emotionally—to find out!)

The "Prince/Principality" that has been assigned to you or that is over your area, ie, over your block, your city, your county, etc., is required by *his* boss to keep tabs on you and find out:

Is he or she serious?

Are they growing in the Lord, or stagnant?

Are they developing in the Word or not?

Are they becoming more aggressive or more passive?

Are they planning on moving in the areas of Life the Lord has told them to, or not?

Have they merely read the Word or internalized it and are they <u>applying it</u>?

What has the Lord called them or told them to do?

What is God planning?

Are they active in what God has said or still 'waiting on the Lord'?

Bottom line—<u>are they a threat</u>?

So, since he can *not* read your mind to tell these things, he applies this technique that the Holy Spirit reveals to us here in Prov. 28:16, or what I have come to call *"The Sponge" Tactic.* This is designed to "squeeze" you for a while to see what comes out, **Word**, or Fear.

You would be surprised what comes out of *some* believers…

Some curse, some swear, some cry, some break, some blame the Lord, some fuss at the Lord, some run away, some stop praying and reading the Word, some backslide, some quit, some sin, some, if not most, get confused, some hesitate to do anything for the Lord anymore, etc.

All of this is *exactly* what the Devil and the "*Principality*" want.

And *then*, at that point, there is usually a "**security breach...**"

We start expressing how *bad off* we are, how *scared* we are, how *worried* we are, etc, and talk our *fears and the problem*, rather than God's Word and the answer. And then we also share and blab the info Satan's been looking for and trying to find out.

What do I mean? Only this, that if there is something going on that the Lord has told us to do, we "*blab* it".

"*I don't know why the Lord let this sickness come on me, I thought He wanted me to start **going out and witnessing to people today?***

Or, "*I don't know why the Lord let this sickness come on me, I thought **He wanted me to start going out to visit the hospitals and pray for the sick with Sister Wilson every Saturday?**" Or,*

"*I don't know why the Lord let the devil attack my finances, especially **since He told me to give to that ministry regularly?**" OR,*

*"I don't know why the Lord let them change my hours on my job like that, especially **since He told me He wanted me to start a ministry to the needy?** He knows I can't do it now..."*

Usually we run and tell other people and he (Satan or one of his demons) ease drops.Ecc.10:20b. And after we finish whinning, complaining and blabbing,

Now that spirit knows *exactly* what *he needed* to know or wanted to find out. Such as…

A. What you were doing for God.

B. What the Lord TOLD you to do.

C. He knows now where you were going to do it.

D. Whom the Lord told you to do it with, and for, also when.

E. Then it wants to get you wondering who did this to you, so that you come to a screeching halt.

F. He wants to weaken your resolve to get it done.

G. Wants you to wander around in spiritual circles wasting time.

H. When you blab, he receives from you instant access into what God has told you to do, and he gains time to go forth and set up 'spiritual road blocks' against you, so that when you finally do wake up and become obedient to what the Lord said, this **Prince** has had *plenty of time* to build up and put in place further spiritual "road blocks" to slow you down, stop you, make you wonder, and send you through this whole process all over again.

*"Was that really **God** that told you to do that? Nawww, it was probably just your flesh cause if it was really God, would it be this **hard**?*" The same technique he applied against Eve.(*"Yea, hath God said?"*) <u>*Did He really say that to you? Awww, that was probably just 'you'. That wasn't God!*</u> Some of us fall for it and then we quit, but the Word says in Phillipians 2:13. **"For it IS God which *worketh in you,* both to *will* and to *do,* of <u>His</u> good pleasure"!**

<u>We trust the Spirit of God more in OTHER people than we do in ourselves!</u>

Sometimes we are so afraid of being "wrong", we don't allow ourselves the opportunity to be…right

Meditate on these things…

The Warrior's Agenda Combat Study Guide—Part 2, by David M. Humphrey Sr, thewarriorsagenda.com, ©Copyright 2003

Satan's Tactics:

The Strategy of Confronting and Defeating a Prince...

Proverbs 14:28...

Proverbs 25:15

Satan's Tactics:

...In the Want of People is the Destruction of the Prince... Prov. 14:28 (B)

What does this verse mean for us in regard to our topic?

In relationship to Spiritual Warfare and Spiritual Combat, it means that in the *want* or *desire* of the people to be *free* of what ever it is Satan has used to keep them in bondage, is the "destruction" of the Prince. In your strong desire to be *free* through the Word of God, is Satan's *destruction*. The destruction of whatever that Demonic or Satanic Prince was trying to do or to use to control YOUR life.

Ever notice how things seem to change and you get a 'break through' when you get *focused* or 'desperate'?

You stop watching TV. You stop calling your favorite girlfriend to gossip. You turn down a plate or two, or three! You pray like you used to, you commit solidly to the things of God.

"*Girllll!*, I'll talk to you later, this thing is getting *serious,* and I got to hear from God!" You get focused, you get serious, you get desperate, and sometimes, you even get "mad"...

In other words, there is some thing that is applicable in the Word of God that I have come to call **"The Law of Spiritual Violence"**.

We see this principle spread through out the Word and talked about even by the Lord Jesus.

Proverbs 11:16: "A gracious woman retaineth honor, and strong men "retain" riches. The original Hebrew of this verse says in the latter half : *and **Violent** men, win riches.*

What's he saying? There are several valid spiritual principles revealed in this verse, but let us stay with the topic at hand.

This verse, Prov. 14:28 and the following verse are connected and reveal the secret of defeating a Demonic or Satanic Prince and their activity in one's life…

Prov. 25:15: "With **<u>long forbearing</u>** is a *Prince* persuaded, and a soft tongue, breakth the bone…" All of the above scriptures which we have quoted, came from the King James Version. The KJV here retains the 'spiritual' implications of these verses as well as the practical aspects.

Where it says "long forbearing", the original Hebrew says, **"in length of temper"**. So in other words: *In length of Temper is a Prince persuaded…"*

You don't get anything from the devil and his minions by being weak, nice and cowardly—nothing that is but a 'black eye'.

We need to make WAR with the enemy, not peace.

You have to get "mad" at what the devil has been doing to you and has been trying to implement in your life! *"In Length of **Temper** is a Prince persuaded!*

Persuaded to do what??

Persuaded to leave you *alone*, that's what!

Satan doesn't like "resistance". Remember James 4:7? 'Submit yourselves therefore to God, and resist the devil and he will "*flee*" from you.

Passive resistance is not *real* resistance. ***Real*** resistance is when you get aggressive against the devil and his minions.

Spiritual aggressiveness with the Word of God will **drive** the "Prince" away from you. They are not use to that.

We have been miss informed. We've been taught to be meek and mild with each other as Believers, like lambs, as well we should. ***But*** we've been misled to believe that we were supposed to be *meek and mild and subservant* to the "devil" too—and *that* is just plain *wrong*.

We are to be meek and mild when it comes to dealing with each other, but we are to be like the *"Lion of the Tribe of Judah"* when it came to the devil and his demons—*ferocious*!

The Lord Jesus is our perfect example.

He was the Lamb of God, yes. ***BUT*** *everytime* it came to dealing with the devil, He turned from the Lamb of God, into the **Lion of the**

Tribe of Judah! Right up to the point where he submitted Himself to die on the Cross for our sins. BUT, after He was resurrected, you don't find him submitting to the devil, sin, sickness, disease, demons, fear, nor anything else that Hell has anything to do with. Infact, we find just the opposite! The Lord tells the disciples, and us to go into all the world and preach the Gospel, nothing would hurt us and the Gates of Hell would *not* prevail against us. Luke 10:19, Matt. 16:18 & 19.

In other words, here's My Name, Here's My Word, here's My Power, now take it—all of it, and go *destroy all the devil's works* and the very Gates of Hell itself will not be able to prevail against you. In other words, go do what I did! Make life hell for the devil and his messengers and set the captives free! Luke 4:18, Luke Chapter 9 and Chapter 10. Matt 9 and Chapter 10:7 & 8!

God *never* designed that Satan and his Princes would make your life Hell on earth, it's supposed to be the otherway around!

How do you defeat a Prince, if you discern one operating in your life?

1. Get angry about it! The Lord Jesus got angry about Satan's thieves being in the Temple, John 2:13-17. He became indignant with the *zeal* of God. That's what *you* have to become when Satan attacks you and your family, become **indignant!**

2. Have a strong desire and determination to be "free" of this attack, what ever it is. Prov. 14:28 KJV. In this is a key to the "destruction of the Prince"...

3. Speak to the Prince and **Command** him to cease and desist and depart! This lets him know that *"you* know" who you are, and that you know that you have authority *and* power over *him* in the Lord Jesus Christ. Matt 16:19, 18:18

4. Stand Your Ground! Remember Prov 25:15! In **Length of Temper** is a Prince *persuded!* That's what the Lord Jesus was trying to teach us through the story (*true* story) of the widow and the Unjust Judge! This was not talking about a Believer and God! Our Heavenly Father is *not* an *UnJust Judge! Satan* is the one who is **Unjust!** *Get it?* This is a story is about a **Believer** and **Satan!** And about how *Satan got scared and said,* **"I better do what this widow woman wants lest she come at the last and "may be assaulting me!"** (Wuest Translation Luke 18:1- 8).

"..lest she give me intolerable annoyance and *wear me out by her continual coming { in 'Length of Temper, remember?},* or at the very last she come and *rail on me* or, <u>assault</u> *me,* or, **strangle me."** *Amplified* ***Bible, Luke 18:1-8***

So, as you can see, our Lord Jesus is *not* talking about God as an *Unjust Judge*? First, our God is *not* unjust, and second, when was the last time you heard about the Lord getting scared that someone was going to 'assault Him' or 'strangle Him"?

Yeah, but Brother Humphrey, why would the devil or his Prince, be scared that I could "strangle" 'them'?

Because you can!

What!!! What in blazes are you talking about?

He Attacks Your Money So You Attack His…

Not physically, but spiritually, by sufficating them with the Word and closing down and destroying their money making operations. Satan needs money to keep his drug industry, his pornography industry and his abortion industry running. Did you ever stop to think about the fact that his people and operations need money to keep things running just like YOU do! Allow the Holy Spirit to train you to begin to think "strategically"…

The Lord Jesus Christ said in Matt 16:19 "I give *you* these Keys of the Kingdom of Heaven…what ever *you Bind* on Earth, will be *Bound* in Heaven, and what ever *you Loose* on Earth, Shall be Loosed in Heaven…" Then, just in case you didn't believe Him, He said it *again*, in Matt. 18:18. Then when He ascended to Heaven, He *left us* the Keys here! *What have you been doing with your Keys!*

Satan is scared to death that you will use them to "strangle" his operations!

"Ok you evil *Prince*, trying to attack my car, shut down my business, disrupt my ministry, attack my finances, over throw my job, destroy my family, destroy my marriage, steal my (God-given dreams), steal my health, kill my peace of mind, joy and happiness, etc.—*I* **BIND all your operations in my neighborhood!Now!** *I strangle your finances, just like you did mine! I command that the Angels of God, go and go NOW to bring Policeman, plainclothes and uniformed, across the path of EVERY MAJOR DRUG DEAL and planned immoral or criminal activity SCHEDULED TO TAKE PLACE WITHIN A 50 MILE RADIUS OF MY HOME—NOW!And I bind all your operations in my area and your money NOW!* IN THE NAME OF THE LORD JESUS CHRIST, UNTIL YOU LOOSE MY MONEY! MY

HEALTH, MY MARRIAGE, MY BUSINESS, MY MINISTRY, MY LIFE!" Etc, etc, and whatever else in your life.

*Wow! But Brother Humphrey, can we **do** that?*

Ofcourse you can! Why do you think the Lord Jesus said, "WHAT<u>EVER</u>" you bind on Earth! He certainly was not talking about binding up the things of God! And frankly, there isn't anything else *to bind up*, except what the *devil* is doing!

So, shut down his operations! You're God's "Policeman". You have a *right* too!

You don't get *your* money? Then, bless God, Satan doesn't get *his*!

You've got more Authority than you've ever realized—*use it!*

Ok, then, after he looses my money Bro. Humphrey, do I "loose" his operations again?

Heck no! You keep them bound! That's the price he must pay for attacking your finances, in the first place! Ex. 22:5 & 6. He was tresspasing. Besides, he has no business operating drugs, or prostitution, or liquor stores, or porn shops, abortion clinics, etc. in your neighborhood ANYway! No! Leave them <u>bound</u>! And tell that Prince if he EVER trys to do that with your money, or health, or

family, or marriage or ministry, or job, etc, again, next time you're not going to stop at 50 miles around your home, it will be 150!

Be aggressive. When he hits you, you hit him back—*harder* with the Word and the weapons of your warfare. You can do more than just *pray*—COMMAND! See Mk. 11:23, Josh. 10:12, Ecc. 8:4, Rom. 4:17, Matt. 17:20, Lk. 17:6. Matt 21:21.

If he decides to test you to see if you *mean* it, hit him again, **harder,** till he *knows* you *mean* business and that you are not **playing,** and then he will back off. Remember: *"In Length of Temper" is a Prince persuaded..."*

5. Pray in **Tongues** about the *Prince*. Pray in Tongues—**Hard, Fast and Loud.** Why? Because this not only *charges you up*, (Jude 20) but it *stirs up* the Gift within you, that Paul talked about. He commanded us by the Holy Spirit to *'stir' up* the gift within us. No where does it say the Lord will do it *for* you. The Lord, *through Paul*, told *us* to do it.

In addition, praying in Tongues this way, actually *stirs up* the "fight" within you too. Praying in Tongues this way stirs up within us a *Spirit of Boldness* and *a Spirit of Power*. 1 Tim.1:7 & 8. It will begin to melt away any feelings of weakness or timidity and release the Gift and the Power and the "Lion of the Tribe of Judah" within you and the

'Prince' will begin to cease operations and flee back into the darkness

where he belongs…

Staying Well Oiled and Ready...

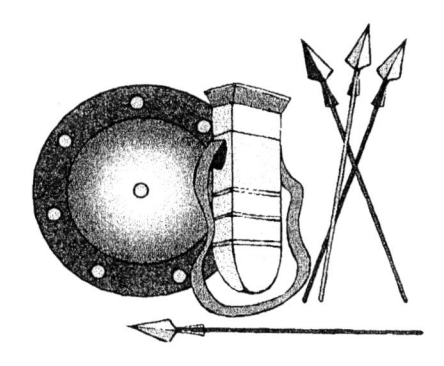

The Power and Necessity of Living a Holy Life

During ancient times of Kings, Queens, and Warriors, when men (and women) were required to wear armour into battle, it was necessary to 'oil' ones' armour and weapons regularly. This kept the leather of your belt, buckles and straps which held up the armour fitting properly and not loose. It kept the leather parts from cracking and fraying, or worse, snapping and breaking off in the middle of a battle. It kept the leather grip with which one held their shield, supple and strong so that even in the most ferocious battle, the grip would not split and the shield would not go spinning away in the heat of battle and leave the warrior defenseless.

It kept the leather 'girdle' around the waist, or what we would call today, the "belt" which held the sword and scabbard, from dry-rotting and falling uselessly into the sand or dirt while running, jumping, fighting or manuevering.

It kept the metal Breastplate, the Shield itself, the Sword and the Spearhead and Javelin, from rusting and becoming corrupted, weak and useless…

Holiness is the Anointed *'Oil'* we must rub our armour down with daily. It helps our Weapons of War to retain their 'sharpness' and their 'edge'.

Like falling alseep on duty, the greatest sin a warrior could engage in in ancient days when in the service of his King, was not taking care of his weapons. Because a rusty weapon was a weak weapon, that the enemy's weapon could slice clean *through*. Every warrior's position was vital to the execution of the over plan of the field generals. One rusty weapon could lead to the untimely death of a solider in a critical position. If he fell, it could open up an entire flank to enemy troops who could then surprise attack and destroy unsuspecting friendly troops from the rear.

An entire battle and even a war could be lost, because of the carlessness of one man…

> *"Follow peace with all men, and holiness, without which no man shall see the Lord..." Heb. 12:14.*

"Holiness" is as vital for us today as "oiling" weapons and armour was to the Warrior-Kings of yesterday.

To deal effectively with **Principalities and Powers,** we must *be* and *have* Holiness as a vital part of our lives. It is the 'oil' by which we as Kings and Priests and Kingdom Warriors keep our armour strong, and fresh, supple and ready for attack or defense today.

As proper oiling kept the quality and the edges of ancient warriors sharp, so does holiness for *us*. Infact, the oiling of weapons is so essential, most quality swords, spears and other metal weapons you buy from accomplished armourers are still <u>oiled</u> and wrapped before they are packaged and shipped, to this day.

In order to effectively deal with a **Prince**, holiness is essential.

In spiritual combat it is required that you live a holy life.

Sin, vulgarity, lying, stealing, jealousy, envy, malice, lasciviousness, lust of the flesh, anger, foul language, back-biting, and all the other works of the flesh will make you useless and ineffective in combat.

Your commands to the devil and prayers to the Lord will die and wither on the vine.

Too many Christians today have been unproductive, powerless, weak and ineffective.

Without Holiness, (and I'm not talking about a denomination, but a daily *Lifestyle* required of *every* Believer) your Sword will not even have a point on it. It will be like hitting the devil with a popsicle stick. Your Shield will not protect you but will cave in under Satan's hammering blows.

Your Breastplate of Rightouesness will dent and warp under his constant pressure.

Your Helmet will stay on, but be crushed on one side and will be ill-fitted and constantly lean on the other.

Your Shoes will not fit properly and will be constantly loose and threaten to slip off your feet.

Whoa Bro. Humphrey! I thought you were going to be building me up in warfare and what to do! Man, you're starting to depress me!

No, this isn't meant to depress you. But it *IS* meant to wake you up to the realities of Combat. And the necessity of you playing your part—*properly.*

This is not a game folks. This IS Combat!

Many Christians think they can walk around and live any old way, as long as it's 'not too bad'. Well, I'm here to tell you, infact I am *required* to tell you—it ain't that way!

God is Serious.

Satan is Serious

WE have to get ***Serious!***

If you play around with sin or an ungoldy attitude, you negate your own ability over the enemy.

How so?

If you run around telling *lies*, even so called 'little white lies', you *negate* your own girdle or "*Belt of Truth*".

The "Belt of Truth" is what holds up your **Sword!**

If you purposly go around lying you "rip" your own *Belt* off!

The Belt of Truth is what *supports* the **Word of God** (*Sword of the Spirit*) in your Life!

Satan is the father of all *lies!* So if you go around lying, you have just *given over your Belt of Truth to the enemy!* You have just "short-circuted" your own access to God's *Power* in your life! Stop that! How can He *empower* the words of a *consistant liar*?

Jonah 2:8 says: **They that give heed to <u>lying vanites,</u> forsake (Heb. relenquish, forsake, leave, and refuse) their own mercy.**

*Ok, now Bro. Humphrey, what does **that** mean???*

I'll tell you.

It means that if you give heed to "lying vanities" you forsake or refuse, or relenquish your "*own*" mercy. The word for mecry here means "lovingkindness bestowed on someone", the "Favor of God," etc. Or we could put it this way, if you listen to and obey Satan's promptings, you "forsake and get out from under the protection, the flow and the Favor of God's lovingkindness, *and restrict* your *own access* to His Power" and it's ability to flow productively *through you*!

Are you still saved?

Yes, but you need to act like it.

Does God still love you?

Yes, but you need to act like you *appreciate* His love, by doing what *He* says, and *not* what Satan and his crew say.

Here's what happens.

Even though we're talking about lying in particular here, this goes for any area of life in which you are not mindful of living holy…

You challenge a *Prince* in your life, or, better yet, he's already challenged *you*. It can be in finances, health, job, career, ministry, family, marriage, home life, loved ones, your mind, etc.

You endeavor to speak the Word, and come against him. You try everything, but nothing's working. You wonder, why Lord? What's going on? He's still there.

But earlier that day, you bad-mouthed somebody, you envied them, or cut them down when you had the chance because of what they did or said to you. You felt they *deserved it*.

Or, you may have faced a totally different situation. You may have felt under pressure for one reason or another regarding your job or work or finances. You were asked a question, and you *lied* about it. Maybe to impress someone. Maybe to get them off your back. Maybe because you didn't like them, they were getting on your nerves and you just wanted to shut them up, or maybe it was a situation where you were afraid of some one who held authority of one type or another and you felt pressured to tell them *something*, so you decided to tell them "something"—*anything* but the truth.

Then the **Prince** comes up against you.

You start to speak the Word, but then…

You suddenly remember what you said, or what you did that you *know* was not pleasing to the Lord.

Some people stop and repent right then and there, which is good.

Some people try to ignore it and go ahead and speak the Word anyway, ignoring what they had said or did, and the Word comes out with no power...

Now, we must stop here and mention another *tactic* of the enemy in order to be extremly balanced in our training, and that is this. *If you have repented of your sin, slip, fall, etc, do NOT let Satan beat you over the head with the guilt of it. Never let him oppress you with a past sin that you have already confessed to the Lord and asked forgiveness for! That will weaken your weapons and armour just as badly as unconfessed sin!*
Why? Because condemnation will short-circute the Power in you too. Why? Because when you condemn yourself you don't allow yourself to have any confidence toward God. In other words, you stop your "own" Faith from working! And the Word says "But without Faith it is impossible to please Him." Heb. 11:6.

Ok, what's the point.
Only this, the Word says that a **Prince,** when he confronts you, seeks to short circuit your Faith, *purposefully*, as a 'tactic'. Either by getting you to step out of leading a Holy Life on purpose (and then not admit it), **OR,** by condemning you for something that you have **ALREADY** been forgiven for, but haven't forgiven <u>yourself</u> for yet. Always remember to forgive *yourself*, because the Lord

will, and *has*, if you have been sincere. Either way, they prevent you from using your weapons and armour effectively.

Make sense?

Here's a passage of scripture that may help you to understand it better. I John 3:18-21 & 22. Let's look at verses 20 & 21.

(20) For if our hearts condem us, God is greater than our hearts, and knoweth all things. (21) Beloved if our hearts **condemn us <u>not</u>, then have we 'confidence' toward God!**

The Lord Jesus Christ has paid for *ALL* of our sins, once and for all, past, present and future. I John 1:9, Heb.8:12, Heb.10:16-17 You have to *know* that and rest in that *confidence* of heart when you go against a *Prince* or any other spirit in Satan's regime with rank.

And at the same time realize that we can *not* take sin lightly (or any other way for that matter), but must lead Holy and Righteous lives. We must wipe ourselves down with the Oil of Holiness daily and allow that Oil to strengthen us and maintain the sharpness of our weapons and the strength of our armour…

A Word of Wisdom About…

The Law of Momentum...

Every one that has ever had to get behind a friend and push his or her car can tell you that it is much easier to push a car that is *moving* and has some *'momentum'* than it is to push a car that has completely *stopped*.

The same thing is true in your spiritual life. It is MUCH *easier* to *keep* yourself motivated while doing the Lord's work. And doing your reading, Bible study, praying, meditating, confessing etc., than it is to 'jump start' yourself from a *'dead stop'*, spiritually.

If you stop reading, meditating, praying, studying, confessing the Word and going to church, you become weak and vulnerable.

Satan knows this, and has had thousands of years to observe this in the lives of millions of humans. So, his strategy and tactic is, once you get started and are really *fired up*, is to tire you out and to *slowwww youuuuu downnnnnn*...

Or...

Trip You Up...

Or...

Distract You...

Or...

Try to *Intimidate* You...

The reason is to always try to *stop* your *forward* momentum.

Have you ever noticed that sometimes things start to go *real well* for a while, prayers get answered, bills start getting payed, the devil gets driven off, you start feeling better, you start hearing from the Lord more—sometimes even *really clear.* But then, after a while, things start to gradually seem to slow down. The blessings seem to start slowing down, not coming as quickly as they did before. Your prayers don't seem to get answered *quite* as quickly as they did before. And you still hear from the Lord, but it doesn't seem to be quite as quickly nor as *clearly* as you did there for a while?

You may even feel at a loss as to why it happened, or what to do about it…

Many times this is because we have lost our *"momentum"*. Momentum is what David had when he faced Goliath in 1 Sam. 17:48. As Goliath rose to begin to approach David, the Bible says that at the exact same time, David hasted and *ran* toward Goliath and the Philistine Army. Then, *while* he was running toward the giant, he pulled out his sling shot, loaded a stone and then *slang it* at Goliath and hit him dead center in the forehead.

The stone *sank into the* giants' forehead and he fell flat on his face to the earth. **But** the Bible says in vs 51 that David *ran* **again**! He *kept* his **momentum going** until he got up to the giant, drew out the giants' sword, and cut Goliath's head off with his own sword!

Like David, do you '*kill*' your giant, *or* do you just 'knock him out'?

Sometimes as believers when we get fed up and decide to face our giants, we pull out the 'stone' of the Word of God, put it in our 'slings'—our mouths, and we *sling it—speak it*—at our enemy Satan, hit him in the head and—***boom!*** He hits the ground, we rejoice, we praise God, we celebrate and tell our friends, high five each other and congradulate ourselves. Gradually we stop *reading* as much as we did.. Gradually we stop *confessing the Word as much and as often* as we did.. Gradually we stop praying or speaking the Word as *intensely or as aggressively* as we did…

Like we've seen in our previous illustrations, we get a bit distracted, sometimes with "good things" which the Lord has blessed us with. We slow down, and we don't notice till it's too late, that the blessings start to slow down *too!* Why? Because we walked away thinking that the 'giant' was dead, when in reality all we did was *knock him out.* ***And***, when *you slow down* on doing the right things, then the *blessings* **keep pace with your obedience** to God and what He's told you to do. And mean while, while we were busy *celebrating*, the giant woke up and, like Arnold Schwartzenagger in the movie 'The Terminator', It said: ***"I'll be baack…"***

When we first started, it was like pushing a stalled car—*hard.* But the more determined we got to "do" this Word thing. Gradually, slowly, the easier it got, because we were *determined*.

However, sometimes, after we get the car 'rolling' so to speak, we want to 'take it easy'. When the first few blessings start to roll in after all our 'hard work' we want to relax a bit and 'chill out' and 'enjoy the fruit of our labor of faith'.

We Want To Coast…

But the problem is, when you are pushing a car on a 'flat surface', the moment you stop *'pushing forward'*, the car starts to *'slow down'*. Yes, it will coast for a while, but shortly there after, it will come to what the world calls a ***dead 'stop'***. Then, it takes what feels like *'twice'* as much effort to get it started and moving again!

Maintain Your Forward Momentum!

Be like David—once you have *wounded* the giant, *don't stop!* Go all the way and *kill* the thing with the Word of God!

No! Don't stop when things start to get a *little* better. No, don't even slow *down*! The giant's *'wounded'* when you start to see some things improve a little bit, but it's not 'dead', and always remember. *A <u>wounded</u> animal can be one of the most dangerous animals there is!*

Let's don't *coast.* **Drive the Word** home into your situation, not *just* until you see some movement and *improvement*, but until the thing is completely *finished* and completely ***gone!***

So remember that the **'*Law of Momentum'*** is an interesting one. Don't stop until it—the problem—is completely gone!

Also, be aware that just before your greatest *victory* may come your *scariest* and *hairiest* moments.

When the giant Goliath fell, he fell on his face, so that means he fell ***forward.*** Sometimes even *after* you know that you have 'killed' the giant it may look like he's still *coming toward you, coming at you.* But **stand your ground,** because sometimes it's only the *momentum of the 'giants' fall'* which makes it ***look like*** he's still coming at you or that the problem or situation is getting worse, when in reality, he's already *dead* and is on his way, face first, to the ground. And shortly there after he and his problems fade away…

Going on the Attack...

Now that you have learned the neccessity and the importance of maintaining Forward Momentum, let's combine this with learning the Principles and Forms of Attack...

As Christians, we should all know that we 'do' have weapons with which we can 'attack' the enemy. Let's take a look at them...

Our Weapons and Modes of Attack

Our Weapons...

Aggressive Prayer...(Binding AND Loosing) Matt 16:19, 18:18

The Word... Heb 4:12, Jer 20:9, Jer 23:29

The Blood of the Lord Jesus... Rev. 12:11

The Word of Command... Josh. 10:20, Job 22:28, Ecc.8:4, Mk 5:28,41 Mk 11:23, Rom. 4:17, Matt. 17:20, Matt 21:21, Lk. 17:6

The Name of Jesus... Phil 2:10, Mk 16:17,

Confession Based on the Word... Rev. 12:11

Methods of Delivery...

ABP: Attack(ing) by Prayer--John 15:7,16:23, Mark 11:24,Matt. 18:19, 21:21

ABB: Attack(ing) by the Blood--Ex.12:13,23, Rev.12:11,1:5

ABC: Attack(ing) by Command--Job 22:28, Ecc. 8:4, Matt 17:20, Josh. 10:12,Luke 17:6, Matt 21:19-20,Mark 11:23,Rom. 4:17, Luke 10:19

ABd: Attack(ing) by Binding--Matt.16:19, Matt.18:18

ABL: Attack(ing) by Loosing—Matt 16:19, Matt 18:18

ABLH:Attack(ing) by Laying On of Hands--Mark 16:17,18 & 20, Matt. 10:8, James 5:13-15

ABN: Attack(ing) by The Name--John 14:14, Mark 16:17, Phil. 2:9,10, Luke 10:17, Acts 3:1-6, Song of Sol. 1:3

ABP: Attack(ing) by the Pheoma Word of God-Rom 4:17

ABW: Attack(ing) by The Word—Jer. 23:29, Jer. 5:14, Ezk. 28:18, Psa 103:20, Eph 6:17, Heb 4:12

Attack By Prayer

In terms of this class, we are looking at prayer as a 'weapon'. As a weapon it is likened to a 'spear'. Long, penetrating, dangerous to the enemy, damaging, swift, and when in action—beautiful to behold.

If you have ever seen a 'Kung Fu' movie or video, then you have observed what a deadly weapon a spear can be in the hands of someone who *knows* what they are doing with it.

That's how good and dangerous you should be with your prayers. Your 'Spear of Prayer' is a far reaching weapon.

Prayer in and of itself is a means of fellowship, communication and even worship, when it comes to our relationship with the Lord, and nearly every Christian in the world is aware of *that* aspect of prayer. ***But***, since this is a class on 'Tactical Spiritual Warfare', let's look at a side of prayer as a 'weapon' against the enemy, that most believers are *not* aware of.

Aggressive Prayer is a very Powerful weapon against the enemy. Examples of David's use of the "Spear of Prayer" are found in the Psalms. Let's take a look at David's use of 'aggressive prayer', shall we?

Turn in your Bibles to the following references. Psalm 18:39-44, Psalm 35:1-6, Psalm 70:1-3, Psalm 71:13 (Lit. Hebrew:*Let them be confounded, shamed and consumed and finished off that are adversaries, **satans, to my soul:** let them be covered with reproach and dishonor that seek my hurt, and evil.*)
Psalm 109:29, Psalm 140:9&10, etc…
These are just some of the ***aggressive prayers*** that David prayed. Sometimes we breeze right through these passages and think that David had no concept of his 'spiritual enemies' and that is not true. He was well aware of them and the true nature of what we read here is directed not merely at his natural *human* enemies, *but*

his spiritual ones too! If we are wise warriors, we will do no less than he did, and with the Blood of Jesus now, and the Name of Jesus, we can be twice as effective as he was…

Attack By the Blood

The Lord Jesus Christ shed His Blood for us, but few of us have really understood what this means. As Beleivers we have all *respected* the Blood, but not many of us have really comprehended It, as well as It's pheonominal benefits. Attack with it.

The Problem

Many of us have a problem with our conscience. For some of us, things that we have repented of still haunt us. For some, even things that we have repented of *years ago.* Almost on a regular basis Satan shows up with a huge bag of condemnation and starts 'sprinkling' us with thoughts, doubts, images and feelings of guilt. And we repent, again…again…again…and again.

But Brother Humphrey, shouldn't we repent for things we've done wrong?

Ofcourse we should. But not for the *same* thing over and over 15 years *after* you have stopped doing it! This hinders your prayer life! This is one of the "weights" that the Apostle Paul warned us to "lay aside", in Hebrews 12:1.

*"Wherefore seeing we also are compassed about with so great a cloud of witnesses, <u>let us</u> **lay aside every weight**, and the sin that doth so easily beset us, and <u>let us</u> run with patience the race that is set before us."*

Weights Slow You Down

Notice. Paul makes a distinction here between 'weights' and *sin.* A weight is not sin. Paul puts them in two different catagories, otherwise this verse would read, "..and let us lay aside every sin, and the sin that doth so easily beset us." There would be no need to say that when he could have just said, "lay aside every *sin*", period. And be done with it. No, he draws a very pertinent conclusion and says: *Drop* the weights, *stop* the sin.

Sin you kill. Weights you *drop*. If you are sinning, stop it *now,* don't wait, don't play with it, don't cuddle it—kill it, ie., ***STOP DOING IT!***

That clear enough?

Ahh, now but weights on the other hand are much more subtle. In a race it's easy to tell if you're 'off track', because you can see the road and know if you leave the beaten path and veer off (into sin). But a *weight,* can be so very subtle because of the fact one is totally unaware that he or she is even *carrying* it!

And in a race, it's like an extra jacket or sweater that we had forgotten we were wearing. Or worse, find out that someone slipped 'rocks' inside our pockets.

But no one would ever run a race like that would they?

Many of us do it every day, without a clue…

The Power of a Clear Conscience

But Brother Humphrey I thought we were studying 'modes of attack' and how to attack the enemy by the Blood of Jesus?

We are, but in the military, before you fire some wepons at your enemy, you have to have a very good and *solid* stance. Otherwise an *unstable stance* will prevent you from firing the weapon accurately and you'll miss the target every time, and the enemy will escape, only to come back and attack you again.

The Blood of the Lord Jesus Christ is such a Weapon—so is the Name.
But check your stance.

In this Warfare that we are engaged in it is supremely important that you have a little thing called *confidence*. This little thing is so vital to your Warfare, that without it, you'll never be fully effective in the Body of Christ. And in addition, whenever Satan needs an ego booster because some other Christian beat him up with the

Word, he'll come to your house to beat *you* up, so he can feel like a devil again.

This little thing called confidence is so important that Paul tells us in Hebrews 10:35 to *"Cast not away your confidence..."* Why? Because *"it hath great recompense of reward"*!
One translation says: *"...it hath MEGA recompense of reward".* (Exegesis Bible)

Ok, now. Let's tie all this together.

If Satan is able to freely *hammer* your conscience with the memories and feelings of guilt from past sins, he can 'weigh down' your prayer life, and instead of coming 'Boldly to the Throne to obtain grace to help in time of need' Heb. 4:16, bearing the Perfect Blood of the Lord Jesus Christ Who has 'purged you from your sins.' Heb 1:3. You'll come with guilt.
What's the difference?

Instead of coming with the Blood of the Lord Jesus on your mind as the preeminent thing and thereby reminding the Father and yourself of what **The Lord's Blood** has done *for you...*

You'll come timidly with your own *sin* on your mind, reminding the Father and yourself *of your past failings.*

The first one *exhalts* the **Father, Son and Holy Spirit** through the **Blood** with what They have done *for you.*

The second one exhalts **Sin, Satan, his kingdom** and what he has done *to you.*

If you have sinned, *repent!* Once you have, move on! *Don't* keep reminding Father of your *sin!* He does NOT want to remember it! (Heb. 10:17!) He does NOT want you to remember it either! (Heb. 8:12).

Sometimes we seem to forget that we are *not* Old Testament saints! Our sins are not merely "covered" by the Blood of the Lord Jesus Christ. Under the Old Testament that's what the blood of bulls, goats, sheep and Red Heifers did. It merely 'covered' their sins. That's why the High Priest had to go in once a year EVERY year and offer the same blood, for the same sins, including his own, because the blood of these animals could never ERASE, PURGE and REMOVE the sins of the people—it could only *'cover'* them. (Heb. 9:1.)

If sin stinks in God's nostrils (and it does) which would smell better? Sin that has been 'covered' or sin that had been totally *"removed"*?

The blood of bulls 'covered' the sins of Old Testament saints, but **the Blood of Jesus**, via the New Testament, which is built upon BETTER promises—*destroys sin!* (Heb. 8:6, 12-13, Heb. 9:13 & 14, 25-26)

Is that an excuse to sin? *No! To the contrary! "How shall we that are DEAD to SIN live any longer therein?"* Romans 6:2.

What's the point? Don't sin! Stop it, and Satan can't condemn you! We have defeated *ourselves*…in many cases. How? Because we have concentrated so much on "sin" that by our focus on *it,* rather than the *Power of the Blood of Jesus OVER it*, and the *grace of God* OVER it, that inadvertantly we gave *it* power over *us*!

The Word says, that where sin did abound, *Grace* did much *MORE* abound! But when we pray to our Father, do we pray more like *Old Testament* saints rather than *New Testament* ones? Do we concentrate first on our *sins and our failings,* rather than the Grace of God? Do we exhalt and put before the Face of God, **His Grace**

and the Blood of Jesus, *or* how we failed, messed up and let the Devil decieve us—*first.*

But Brother Humphrey, aren't we supposed to repent for our sins? Ofcourse you are—but you should have done that ***the moment you sinned, not 'waited' until you get into your prayer time with the Father!***

First off, you *should not sin—period. Let's get that* <u>straight</u>. *But if you do, we have an advocate, 1 John 2:1-2 and 1 John 1:9.* Second, once you have sincerely confessed that sin, The Lord Jesus Himself uses **His own Blood to <u>purge us clean of that sin, and from ALL unrighteousness!</u>** And if that's true—and it is—then why do you and I act like He's a liar and purged us from "some" unrighteousness, but not *ALL*?

We have to *Stop* believeing our 'feelings' and believe the *Word!* You'll never have any confidence toward God if you spend 5 hours a day repenting over and over again for the same thing you did day before *yesterday, or ten years ago.* No Army ever won a battle marching two miles forward, then *five miles backward*—you'll never get anywhere that way! At that rate you, and I will *never* be a *threat* to the enemy, we'll just be his *entertainment!*

*"Look at those dumb Christians, they don't even know the difference between 'conviction' and 'condemnation'. They're not going to be a problem. We won't have to fear **their** prayers. Our little friend, the 'Spirit of Condemnation' will remind them so much of their failures that their prayers will be more 'sin' conscious, than Faith and Grace conscious, they will think more*

*about their 'sin', than how the Blood of Jesus has **destroyed it**...Ha! They fell for our very 'first' test! Tell the master not to worry, these Christians didn't even make it past our First Level Demon—Condemnation. They are a push over and will be no problem for us to handle..."*

(Jer. 12:5)

Consider this. When you go into your prayer time to your Heavenly Father, do you concentrate more on your *sin*, or the **Power of the Blood of Jesus**, that has already condemned and destroyed it? Destroyed it SO thoroughly, that the Father said *three times* ,

"And their sin and their iniquities I will remember NO more...
Hebrews 8:12, Hebrews 10:17 and Jeremiah 31:31-34
The Holy Spirit 'Convicts', (John 16:7-9),
But Satan 'Condemns' and the Lord has made us Free from
Satan's Condemnation (Romans 5:1 & Romans 8:1 & 2)

I don't know about you, but I'm like Jeremiah in Jer. 6:11,
"Therefore I am 'full' of the Fury of the Lord; I am weary with holding it in..."

Let's obey the Word of God. Don't attack your brother or your sister in Christ. Don't attack your boss or family members, or Pastor and friends. And no—don't even attack *yourself* and condemn yourself anymore. Let's do what the Word says. Let's attack our *real enemy* and "*execute against him the judgements written...*"

"*...This **Honor** have **all** His saints...*"

...Psalm 149:9...

Remember, you will never receive the abundant Bountifulness of God, nor His Power, by constantly repeating His *enemy's* greatest past *achievements in your life...*

This is the End of Part Two
Coming Soon, the Warrior's Agenda Combat Study Guide Part 3

About the Author…

David M. Humphrey Sr is an ordained minister who has been called to train 'volunteers' in the Body of Christ in the principles of *'Tactical Spiritual Warfare'*. David has been an ordained minister of the Gospel since 1981. He taught his first Bible class at the age of 17 in 1970.

Shortly after she was married, the doctor told David's mother, the late Min. Harriet M. Humphrey, that she would never be able to have children. Though unsaved at the time, she knew enough about the Lord to know where to go when she needed a miracle. She prayed a simple prayer.

'Lord, if you will bless me with a son, I will dedicate him to You…' This was the exact same prayer that Hannah had prayed in I Samuel Chapter 1.

True to her word, she dedicated her only child to the Lord at the moment of his birth, and again, when he turned thirteen years old.

David has known both the joys and scars of Spiritual Warfare. At the lowest point in his life David suffered a series of blows from the enemy, culminating in a heart attack. It was at this crucial point in his life that the Lord spoke to him clearer than He ever had before. He said to David in the middle what would later be diagnosed as 'congestive heart failure': *"Son, Satan is trying to kill you.. And if you die, right now...you'd come to be with Me... Or, you can stay and you can fight..."*

David pondered quickly all the things he knew he hadn't done for the Lord yet. Pondered his life and the fact that he knew he was nowhere near ready to stand before his Lord. Barely able to breathe, much less talk, he forced air into his lungs and said, *"Lord, I'm going to stay and I'm going to fight..."* He then literally rebuked the spirit of Death, and Satan, in the Name of Jesus, and drove himself to the hospital. Ever since that day in 2001, one month before September 11, he has been training the people of God in the Word, per the Lord's direct instructions. The Lord said to David recently:

"Train Me an Army…"

Every major military force in the world has both conventional forces and then *"Special Forces"*. It is David's mission in life to train Believers how to be God's 'Special Forces'—Spirit Led, Word Fed, walking in love with others, but *aggressive* and *effective* against the enemy…

David prays that this Combat Study Guide has been a blessing to you. Please feel free to visit our website: www.thewarriorsagenda.com, or email us at: **thewarriorsagenda@yahoo.com.**

David has been the host of his own Cable TV program, **The Warrior's Agenda Broadcast,** and has taught numerous Bible Studies over the years including classes on Spiritual Warfare at a Study he founded called **The War College.** In 2003 the Lord called David and his wife Velma to learn more about healing, and in obedience to the Lord's leading they moved to Texas early in 2005 and have been studying the Word and learning about God's great moves of power through the early

20th century church. They are currently associated with John G. Lake Ministries.

David's first fiction book, **Dark Things**, a supernatural thriller on Spiritual Warfare in Washington, DC, has received very favorable reviews and has been compared to the works of Mr. Frank Peretti. His book is currently available at a number of Christian bookstores across the country as well as from amazon.com, borders.com, barnesandnoble.com, and books-a-million.com. At the moment, David is working one three other books including, a sequel to his popular book '**Dark Things**' and Part 3 of the current Combat Study Guide…

Notes For Chapter 1:

Notes For Chapter 2:

Notes For Chapter 3:

Notes For Chapter 4:

Notes For Chapter 5:

Notes For Is There Not a Cause:

Notes For Paraclete:

Notes For Boot Camp:

Notes For Special Forces:

Notes For Navy Seals:

Notes For Perimeter Defense:

Notes For Tactics of the Enemy:

Notes For The First Step:

Notes For Believer's Special Forces Creed:

What Do You Know About Satan's Tactics:

Staying Well Oiled and Ready:

Misc. Notes: